The Joyful Woman's Guide to Self-Care

Refresh, Reset, Restore, and Reclaim Your Life

The Joyful Woman's Guide to Self-Care

Refresh, Reset, Restore, and Reclaim Your Life

BY

KANDICE COLE

Published by
Hybrid Global Publishing
301 E 57th Street
4th Floor
New York, NY 10022

Cole, Kandice
The Joyful Woman's Guide to Self-Care: Refresh, Reset, Restore, and Reclaim Your Life
    ISBN: 978-1-951943-79-0
    eBook: 978-1-951943-80-6
    LCCN: 2021916244

Cover design by: Natasha Clawson
Copyediting by: Dea Gunning
Interior design by: Suba Murugan
Author photo by: Terron Cole

Disclaimer: If you know or suspect you have a health problem, it is recommended you seek your medical or mental health professional's advice.

www.kcolewellness.com

CONTENTS

ACKNOWLEDGEMENTS

Books, like children, require an enormous amount of support and love, to bring them to life. I am always humbled at just how much support and love was given to make this book real.

Terron: Thank you for reminding me to practice self- care all of the time when life gets busy. You are a constant support. I love doing life with you.

Inara and Miles: You are the reason why I stay on this self-care journey. You both are my greatest joy, and a constant reminder for me to give myself permission to play more. May you know a life where self -care and rest are the norm.

A special thanks to all of the Publishizer patrons who pre-ordered 100 copies of a book that didn't even exist fully. Without every single one of you this book would not be here.

A very special thanks to:

Felicia Redic
April Frazier-Camara
Shantera Chatman
Shayla Boyd-Gill
Sherri Stewart
Faisal Mohyuddin

Fenesha Hubbard
Louisa Shannon
Polly Kimberly

To everyone who liked a post, read my blogs, watched my videos, and supported my evolving work: Thank you. Without those moments to workshop ideas or get my thoughts out, I would not have made it here. Thank you for showing up and giving me constant encouragement and feedback.

INTRODUCTION

'You don't always have to be doing something. You can just be and that is plenty.'-Alice Walker

I am so glad you are reading this book. Before you start reading, take a deep breath through your nose and then exhale. Do that one more time. Now focus on your shoulders. Are they hunched up or tense? If so, then relax your shoulders. Now, start to move your neck towards your shoulders. Take another breath. Depending on when you are reading this book, you may have just finished a really tough day. You might be starting this in the morning before the busyness of the day takes over. Whenever you decide to start reading this is a good time. Celebrate that you are here reading about taking care of a very important person-You.

Throughout this book, I am going to do periodic pauses like the one above. These pauses take less than a minute, but are a reminder that self- care can be simple and something that can be done all the time. As you read the book, take what you need and release what doesn't fit right now. It really is that simple. Whether you are just starting your self- care journey or looking to expand your existing self- care practices, I know you will find some gems in this book to encourage you along the way.

First things first. Take a moment to notice how you are currently feeling. Take a minute to jot down some words to describe how you feel right now. Be as specific as possible and go beyond happy, mad, sad, and bad. If you are feeling happy, are you feeling confident or hopeful? If your feelings are shifting towards feeling mad, are you irritated or angry?

Declare out loud: **I deserve to take really good care of myself.**

Jot down the first thoughts that pop up into your mind when you say that statement out loud. read it. Regardless of what comes up, don't censor yourself. You might feel excited, hesitant, or completely unsure. Whatever it is, simply observe without judgement.

How do you most want to feel? If you were taking really good care of yourself, how would you feel? Write those answers down, too. And remember to allow what you really want to emerge. Even if you have no idea how, it is important to name how you really want to feel. We will return back to those thoughts as you make your way through the book.

PART 1: REFRESH

MY STORY

I have been obsessed with checklists and planning since I was a young child. Maybe it is because I'm a Virgo. It might be because I am the oldest child or simply because I like being in control. Whatever the reason, I have always loved having a solid plan with all of the details organized meticulously. I remember picking out the colors for my wedding in high school, and I even created a timeline of when I would have children, too. My perfect life checklist went something like this:

- Get college degrees.
- Get a great job.
- Get married.
- Have kids.
- Travel.
- And live happily ever after.

Interesting how the happily ever after didn't happen until I had done so many things. After graduating high school, I started checking things off that list. I graduated from college, being the first person in my immediate family to graduate with Bachelor and Master's degrees. After a rigorous year-long teaching residency in Chicago, I moved to Sacramento and began my teaching career at a newly formed charter school. About three months into that teaching assignment, something did not feel right. I felt off balance, and just felt a general sense of apathy about many things.

Being a first year teacher in a startup school was particularly tough. I had to juggle between finding my balance as a new teacher, while taking on many responsibilities to help create a school culture that was being built from the ground up. It was an exciting challenge that had so many unknown elements. I was working non-stop, often bringing work home and staying up late into the night. When I finally did go to bed, I was absolutely exhausted. This reality was something that I heard other teacher friends experiencing, and I remained hopeful that it would get better. I was a new teacher, in a new city, at a new school. That was a lot of transition and it would take time to find my footing. This was the real world of being an adult, and this beginning phase was just part of the course.

Every morning, I hoped that I would wake up feeling like my regular self. I longed to feel something different. I wanted life to have a flow to it and finally click into place. Instead, I felt like I was running on a treadmill that kept going faster and faster. Every day I woke up, I felt more exhausted. Now a new feeling, sadness, had joined the morning routine. I tried to shake this feeling and convince myself that this too would pass. I read personal development books and listened to uplifting music. I prayed and wrote out positive affirmations on notecards. I even joined the local chapter of my sorority to meet some new people in the city. This feeling of tired sadness lingered like a cloud that steadily hovered over me. The color of my world was getting duller and losing its vibrancy. This was not a part of my checklist and I had no plan for this. I didn't know how to make sense of what was happening to me. Instead of leaning in for support, from those close to me, I isolated myself because I was too embarrassed to share how I was really feeling.

The gap between how I wanted to feel and how I was actually feeling was growing wider day after day. Some days I could shrug it off long enough to focus and do work, but the exhaustion got increasingly worse, and the sadness would linger longer. It was becoming harder to focus and I felt very unmotivated to do anything. I was falling behind with grading papers and organizing my classroom. On the weekends, I only wanted to lay on the couch and watch TV, which didn't help me feel more rested or happy.

I assumed that the source of my unhappiness was this particular teaching job. I started obsessing about switching to a school that was more established and that would offer more support for a fledgling teacher like myself. I thought about moving back to Chicago where I had a strong personal and professional network. I connected these uncomfortable emotions with external situations and desperately wanted relief. Seven months after starting, I officially quit my first teaching job. I partially felt like a failure, but honestly I felt like I could take a breath. I made another plan: Regroup, get back to my regular self and find another teaching job.

I had thought about doing substitute teaching, but decided I needed a break from teaching at least for the rest of the school year. I still wanted to work with kids, so I went back to my babysitting roots and found a job as a nanny for an infant with a really great family. Over the course of a few months, I started to feel like myself again. I was sleeping better. I was journaling every day. I was given a bike and rode to work a few days a week enjoying the scenery. I was also taking walks with the baby almost daily and that lifted my spirits. I started to feel less exhausted when I woke up. I could see and feel glimmers of happiness returning. It was as if a long winter was finally making way for springtime. I felt like myself again, meaning I felt more energized and happy. I checked regroup off of my list along with getting back to my regular self. Now I was ready to get back into teaching.

The following year, I moved back to Chicago excited to start teaching again. I was smarter and wiser this time around. I had a stronger support network in Chicago for navigating the new teacher phase. I found a job at a school where I had previously done student teaching, and was given the space to try new things in the classroom. I taught the entire school year and didn't quit. It had its challenges, but I genuinely enjoyed being in the classroom with my students.

As summer rolled around, I had so much to celebrate. I accepted a new teaching position at my dream school, a place where I had done the majority of my student teaching and where teacher development was a top priority. I dove into professional development opportunities and connected with my colleagues. I ended up teaching for two years at the school, but something started to change in that second year.

I started feeling that exhaustion and sadness that I had felt during my first teaching job. It was not as intense, but it was there pulsing underneath it all. I found myself increasingly doing more work, and staying up later to complete it. We had a rigorous curriculum, and were a high performing school. I once again attributed it to the job and that it was crunch time with assessments. Teaching in a public school is not easy, and retention rates for teachers are pretty low across the country. Maybe I had just picked a profession that was inevitably going to exhaust me. With this realization in mind, I made the decision to leave teaching.

Over the next few years, I explored different routes including consulting, freelance work, and nonprofit management. The same pattern persisted as it related to my energy. I would go full steam ahead and things would be okay for a while. I would throw all of my attention and energy into a project and feel fine. Then, I would sputter out, lose motivation, and feel unhappy. I could push through and get things done, but it was not what I wanted to be the norm. Looking back, I see that I was experiencing burnout, but in the early 2010s that term was not being used like it is today.

It took me a long time to see that a particular job or industry was not the sole cause of my unhappiness and sadness. I had a habit of diving into new jobs and endeavors, without ever coming up for air. I would eagerly put so many things on my plate and then feel the effects later. By the time I noticed how I was feeling, I was so exhausted that I ended up getting sick or missing important deadlines. I didn't understand this pattern until many years later when I started journaling and working with a therapist. Turns out, I was not actually taking care of myself as well as I had imagined. I continued to experience this as I checked things off of that ideal life checklist. I got married. I did some traveling. After being married for six years, we welcomed our first child into the world.

After having my daughter, I was consumed with newborn life and the learning curve of being a first time parent. My husband and I were going through a tough time financially, which meant he was working longer hours to make ends meet. I was completely overwhelmed with motherhood and struggling through postpartum depression. Some days it felt difficult to even get out of bed and take a shower. I felt irritable and sad most of the time.

This felt familiar, but even more intense than before and I wanted to do something different. I knew that I had to disrupt this burnout pattern that had been happening for the past decade. I didn't know what to do quite yet, but I knew that I wanted to be a happy mother, wife, and person in general. Of all the things I had put on my checklist, being happy was not specified. I had assumed that doing certain things would guarantee happiness, but that was not the case. Happiness was about what was going on inside of me, and I needed to focus on that. I didn't know how I was going to do that, but I was ready for a change.

As I became ready, resources started to find me. Kind of like when the student is ready to learn, the teacher appears. Over the course of many years, I would come to understand the importance of a consistent, and varied self - care routine.

It took a lot of things for me to understand the entire process of taking care of myself. There is a lot that happened between where I am now and where I was. And it is a lot of space between where I am currently, and where I want to be in my wellness journey.

This book is about how messy and joyfully worthwhile it is to develop a self- care practice. While it would be nice for everything to work out perfectly when it comes to taking care of yourself, the journey is not linear. It is more like putting together a puzzle. You add a piece here and see if it fits, then you do that over and over again until you create something that is whole. So much of our self -care, or lack thereof, is a result of beliefs, experiences, and societal narratives that we carry with us. It takes a tremendous amount of patience and acceptance to stay committed to self- care.

If you feel resistant as you read this book, know that it is okay. If you feel so exhausted that you can't even imagine being any other way, know you are not alone. I used to have days when I didn't want to get out of bed and wanted to hide under the blankets. I couldn't imagine a day when I would want to get out of bed and actually feel joy and peace constantly. Yet, this morning, I got out of bed and felt good. It took a bunch of small steps (and missteps) to find my way back to myself, but it was a journey worth taking.

Showing up is what matters. You might show up excited or scared, but you still show up. You might show up sad and tired. You might be at one hundred percent or at one percent. You keep showing up because you are that important. And you know what? There is not a finite arrival point on your self- care journey, it's more like milestones and checkpoints that show how you are evolving. You will learn lessons, grow, evolve, and repeat the process over and over as your life changes. Your self- care journey is an ongoing act that requires something different at certain stages of your life. I think making peace with that has been the saving grace for me. I am not the same person I was a few months ago. You are not the same person you were a few months ago. It is up to you to honor who you are becoming instead of trying to force yourself to be something that no longer fits. As I write this book during the pandemic, I know many of you have had to completely rethink your life. You have had to really grapple with what taking care of yourselves really means.

This book is not a cookie cutter step by step process. It is more of a reflective guide to help you move through your own unique way of understanding your self -care journey. That being said, it does not have to be read in order. You can pick whatever chapter seems right for you at the moment. Give yourself what you need, and always trust that you know exactly what you need.

You are a brilliant person who is doing a lot. You have put yourself on the back burner for far too long. You may have started prioritizing your self- care ,but there is more terrain to cover and more to deepen into, too. Coming back to yourself is a journey worth taking. On the other side of the exhaustion is something beautiful. On the other side of the transition is something exquisite. Who you are when you prioritize rest is the truth of who you really are.

I will not make any grand promises about what this book will do for you. My hope is that this book will encourage you to stand in your power, and create a life that is a source of constant nourishment and love.

Find a comfortable spot, get your favorite drink, and get ready to practice self -care all the time.

SELF -CARE VALUES

Values are our North Star. They help us to put things into context and determine what is a priority in our lives. Everything in this book comes from the following core self- care values that I have learned over the years in developing my own self- care practice, and helping other people develop their practices.

1. Practice self- care when you feel good. Self -care is not just reserved for times when you feel exhausted. Practicing self- care is a constant practice, which supports optimal well- being.

2. You are a multidimensional person who needs multidimensional self -care. We will talk about this later in the book but know this: you are a human being with many different aspects of yourself. Self- care is not a singular experience, and it should reflect all of the different parts of who you are.

3. Self- care and fun go hand in hand. Play and creativity are an integral part of a self -care practice. Everything does not have to be so serious. When we embrace play, we open ourselves up to infinite possibilities in our self- care rituals.

4. Self- care can be infused into your everyday routines. Your daily routines provide opportunities for you to practice self- care. Rather than viewing self- care as an additional activity or task, we can start to view self- care as a way of living life.

5. Self- care is how you are, not just what you are doing. How you do something is what matters most. Intentionally focusing on your being is the key to creating self -care practices that matter to you, and that make a difference in your life.

Reflect: What value resonates the most with you?

TYPES OF SELF CARE

Self-care is everywhere these days. The self- care industry is valued at over 400 billion dollars and we are seeing it normalized in the media. But what is self- care? Depending on who you ask, the answer may vary because it encompasses so many products, services, and approaches. Let's explore what self- care actually means when it is detached from money or achievement.

Being present is the first way to practice self -care. Being present and staying present is the foundation of all of our self- care practices. If you can be present and mindful for just a minute, you are practicing self- care. Being present to what is happening in our mind, our life, our body, and our spirit creates moments of clarity that provide relaxation and ease. Being present can feel impossible when so many things are competing for your attention. Self- care becomes a practice in noticing what is here, even when it seems complicated. When I host virtual retreats, I always start with this idea about being present. If you are a busy person, you might have the desire to do it all. You fill your plate and do ambitious things daily because that is the kind of life you lead. We applaud you for that, but when was the last time someone applauded you for taking a break? Or asked if you were going to rest?

I invite you to be present right now. Take a deep, delicious inhale, then exhale letting all of the air out. Take a scan of your body. What parts of your body feel tense? Just notice and be mindful of that. Take another deep breath in and out.

That pause is one simple way to practice self- care in our real lives at any moment. Self- care really is that simple. If you look on social media, there are self- care tips and advice everywhere, which is very overwhelming. It might seem like self -care is just a series of meditation, baths, and candles. It might seem like you need a lot of supplies to have a self- care practice that works. I enjoy all of those self -care practices, but self- care is more than one singular activity. Let's dive into a few definitions of the word to get some insight.

One definition of self- care from the Oxford Dictionary is: 'The practice of taking an active role in protecting one's own well-being and happiness, in particular during periods of stress.'[1] In the book, *How We Show Up*, Mia Birdsong goes deeper into what self- care really is and how it is different from self- soothing. She explains that self- soothing is focused on providing distraction or comfort from difficult times. On the other hand, self -care is things that help you find meaning and support your growth. It is such an important distinction to make between self -soothing and self -care. What we are wanting and needing are moments of nourishment and care.

As I look back at my past experiences, it is clear I was doing a lot of self- soothing. As a result, I was not feeling particularly energized or refreshed, since those things are a byproduct of finding meaning and support.

---

[1] "self care." /www.lexico.com. Lexico, 2021.Web. 27. September 2021.

Quick check in: Take a deep breath. Now, let it go. Have you been practicing self- care or self- soothing? How does it feel when you do one over the other?

Self -care spans a spectrum of practices that we don't normally see on social media or television. Self- care does not mean that you stay positive all of the time. Naming how you feel during difficult times can actually be a powerful form of self- care. Self- care might mean doing things that are uncomfortable like setting boundaries with family (more on that later) that you know will serve you in the future. Sometimes it is about reconnecting to what you know to be true, and letting go of past stories that have limited your belief in your abilities. There are many ways to think about self- care. Remember the self- care values from the last chapter about self- care needing to be multi-dimensional? Here are a few categories to help us broaden our sense of how expansive self- care actually is. This list is not exhaustive but it is a start:

- **Social Self -Care:** Taking care of yourself does not mean that you do it alone. There are times when we have to be in community with someone else or a group in order to better understand ourselves. Sometimes taking care of ourselves means connecting with groups that lift us up and make us feel understood. Social self- care is about connection, and the benefit that connection brings to you and your life. This might look like calling a close friend on the phone or taking a road trip with your family. It could also look like sitting and looking at photos with a family member, or engaging in a Facebook group. When the pandemic happened, we all understood how important social self -care was and craved it in our lives. This caused us to create robust virtual communities and gatherings that filled the need that we couldn't get in person due to lockdowns. Social self- care is not about the extrovert/introvert paradigm. This is more about recognizing the part of ourselves that needs connection with other people. As leadership consultant and change maker Akaya Windwood, said, "Notice you. Notice you among us."[2]

- **Spiritual Self -Care:** When you are in need of grounding or affirmation in your faith, it might be time for some spiritual self- care. Spiritual self- care might coincide with social self- care, or can be spent in solitude. Some people like to call this soul work. This kind of self- care includes going to places of worship, being out in nature, or meditating. This might also mean being curious about a spirituality practice, and trying something new in pursuit of feeling connected to your spiritual self.
- **Creative Self- Care:** This is one of my favorite types of self- care. Creative self- care is focused on activating your creative energy. We are all creative beings and that creativity needs to be cultivated. Many times these activities are centered around

[2] Birdsong, Mia. *How We Show Up: Reclaiming Family, Friendship, and Community.* New York: Hachette Go, 2020. Print.

play, thinking out of the box, or doing things totally unrelated to one another. It is about making space to create new ideas and bring them to life in a myriad of ways. Everything we use was an idea in someone's imagination first. Creativity requires us to do things that are different than how we might normally do things. You might paint, go to the playground, drive a new way to work, or listen to an album in its entirety. We will dive more into this type of self- care later in the book.

- **Emotional Self- Care:** Noticing your emotions is worthwhile work. It is also an important way to be clear about your internal state and to advocate for yourself. This might look like journaling, going to therapy, or setting a boundary with someone. Tending to your emotional landscape might feel daunting, so please make sure to seek out professional help when needed. A great place to start is with naming your feelings in more nuanced ways. Feelings wheels are a great tool to start with if you find it difficult to identify how you are feeling. A feelings wheel is divided into sections of core emotions such as happy, sad, and bad. Once you identify a core emotion, it fans out and includes many adjectives to help sort out how you specifically feel (for example: feeling sad but digging deeper and realizing you feel disappointed.).

- **Workplace Self -Care:** Our jobs are often the cause of a ton of stress. With a new perspective, we can start creating self- care rituals at work instead of thinking we have to wait to do it after we finish our hours. This might look like breaks in between meetings, not checking email after a certain time, or doing certain tasks on a consistent basis during the week without interruption.

- **Physical Self- Care:** This is the most commonly known self- care category, and it includes everything from exercise to nutrition, to taking those warm bubble baths that we see advertised. Physical self- care also includes scheduling routine medical exams, sleep, and stretching, too. Our bodies do so much for us and we need to give it love every chance that we get.

This is not an exhaustive list, but definitely something to take into consideration when thinking about your self- care. Remember, this is just the beginning. The first step is to simply notice yourself. It is important not to neglect certain aspects of yourself that require attention and care. Unfortunately, the term self -care has been overused and turned into a shallow trend that is more about capitalism than wellness. It is all too easy to feel like you are not doing self- care right if it doesn't look a certain way. There isn't one way to do self- care. These are practices and rituals that bring you back to feeling relaxed, refreshed, and happy. It is creating rituals, (which we will talk about later in the book), that energize you and make you feel balanced, even when life is chaotic. With intention, so many actions can be a part of your self- care practice.

As you begin to think about your own self-care, remember that you might be in need of a specific kind of self-care. Take a few minutes and ask yourself:

- What type of self-care am I craving most right now?
- What type of self-care have I not considered or done in a while?

The answer may or may not surprise you. Either way, **you have got to trust yourself.** Trust that you know what you need. Go with that flow, even if it is something new. Allow what you need to change and shift. Listen to what your intuition is telling you, and move towards practices that support that. The world we live in is so loud with information coming at us from all angles. Make sure to turn that noise down and listen to yourself.

As you read and reflect, it is important to affirm what you want. In the next chapter we are going to talk about the guilt we feel when we make time for our self-care. Affirmations help to focus our mind and energy on what we do want, even if our life does not reflect it at the moment. Choose which affirmations speak to you the most, or add your own.

- *Self-care is non-negotiable in my life*
- *I am worthy of being nurtured*
- *I trust that I know what I need*
- *I give myself permission to practice self-care my way*
- *Taking care of myself is top priority*
- *Self-care is fun and joyful*

It takes a bunch of small steps to push back on societal norms that tell us to work without taking breaks and to ignore our needs. These affirmations are simple reminders of what is actually true, even on days when it doesn't feel like it.

Self- care all the time is about choosing yourself, even when it feels difficult. Choose yourself even if the norm is for you not to because you are responsible for so much. You need you more than everyone else needs you. We practice muting that need, that voice, that yearning to take care of ourselves. This is an unfortunate consequence of living in a perpetually busy society. Sometimes self- care is simply this: *to listen to yourself.* To hear what you most need without guilt, without shame, without anything but love. To listen intently with love is a gift.

Reflect:

What kind of self- care do you need right now?

PART 2: RESET

OVERCOMING GUILT

A few months into the pandemic, I needed to get out of the house. I sat alone in my car in the parking lot of a nearby park. I could hear birds chirping and cars driving past. I had my favorite playlist playing softly. I opened up the white carryout box from my local cafe and took a deep breath. The smell of breakfast immediately met my nostrils and sparked joy. I started to slowly eat the breakfast crepe, savoring the saltiness of the ham and eggs against the backdrop of the thin sweet crepe. After a few bites, I took a sip of a chilled mint tea. At that moment, all felt right with the world. All in the middle of a pandemic, where I found myself at home doing remote learning, on more Zoom calls than I could stand, and pregnant during a scary time in the world. Things felt okay at that moment. All of my senses were indulged--tasting the crepe, smelling the food; feeling the coolness of the condensation from the cup; watching outside and listening to music. It looked a little different since we were in the pandemic, but it was a beautiful moment.

For an hour of time and about eleven bucks I had created a self- care moment that I needed. I was so proud of myself. Not just for taking the time, but also for not feeling guilty for doing it. And that was a huge feat for me not to feel guilty about taking time for myself, especially being a parent. I recognized that I needed some time for myself and instead of waiting until I was sick or down, I did something about it much sooner.

A few years ago, this scenario probably would not have happened. I would have overlooked how I was feeling and put my family's need before my own. I would have allowed myself to spiral. I would have tried to do more work or check another email. I would not have told anyone how I was feeling or what I needed. I would have felt an immense amount of guilt, which would have made it really hard to actually engage in self- care. Now, I notice that guilt and I look at it with curiosity, and I understand that guilt is not my story. I am free to tell a new story. You are free to tell a new story.

Guilt is such a tricky feeling. In the Merriam Webster dictionary, guilt is defined as 'feelings of deserving blame especially for imagined offenses or from a sense of inadequacy.'[3] It is interesting that guilt can be about how we feel about something that has not actually happened yet. If you are a recovering people pleaser like me, then you know how enormous guilt can feel. It takes up the whole room and leaves you no space to enjoy your life. You always feel like you are obligated to take care of everyone else first. Sometimes, this feeling is because you feel indebted to someone, perhaps a parent or family member who has done things for you. Other times, you just feel guilty about

---

[3] "guilt." www.merriam-webster.com. Merriam-Webster, 2021.Web. 27. September 2021.

saying no to someone's request because you don't want to be known as being unhelpful. Here are two other reasons why I think guilt becomes our default reaction for some additional reasons.

- We don't know who or what we are without being the helper, which can feel embarrassing, disappointing, sad, or any other intense emotion. Overwhelm has a way of making us avoid the thing we most need to do. And often we are overwhelmed because we are trying to do too many things, and aren't sure where to start.

How we think about ourselves in relation to our self- care, usually involves deprivation. We say things like, if I take care of myself, then I won't have time to help my kids. If I take an hour to do this, then I will have to tell my friend I can't go out. If I tell someone that I cannot do ___, then they will be mad at me. Our self- care is always connected to someone not getting something. It is always attached to this thought that we are depriving someone else of a necessary resource. So, even if you do some self- care, you are anchored by this idea that this action you are doing is connected to hurting, or taking away from someone else. With that negative association, what is the natural response? Of course, you don't want to do anything that will cause that icky feeling. If you find yourself feeling guilty about self- care, especially taking longer stretches of times, know that it is normal. You care a lot about other people around you and don't want to let them down,-which points to your generosity and kind heart. And before you start chastising yourself with thoughts, you know ones like: 'Why am I like this? I can't believe I can't stop doing so much for others. I need to fix this.' This is not necessarily something to fix as much as it is something to shift. Think about it like a car where you have to shift gears. If you drive in one gear it works for certain distances and terrain. When you get to another speed, you have to change the gears. This doesn't mean you have to fix the entire car.

You are shifting and learning to value your self -care in the context of what it adds to your life rather than what you perceive it taking away from someone else. And you might disappoint people. You might make people upset. You might make people have to learn to be independent. And that might feel hard, yet it is much harder to keep holding yourself back. We have to learn to navigate those uncomfortable feelings while we still make choices for our highest good. We think that once we don't feel guilty, we can practice self- care, but we have to practice self- care in order to move through the guilt. And we have to understand that guilt with compassion, the same way we talk to a small child who is having a tantrum. Our guilt responses are pathways to stories and memories that we can observe, reflect on, and release. That releasing allows us to create new pathways that lead us to understanding why we need to nurture ourselves consistently.

I love watching home renovation shows and my latest obsession has been with backyard makeovers. I was watching one show where they were actually building a small office space in someone's backyard which needed electricity. There was a shed they were renovating that had a power outlet. Upon further inspection the contractor realized that the outlet didn't connect to the main electrical unit that powered the house and that it had not been installed properly. He had to dig up the original outlet and cord, then cut it from whatever power supply it was on, then lay new wires deeper into the ground and connect them to the main power supply of the home. This took an additional day to do, but the family would not have to worry about this issue again.

So here we are having to do some digging and rewiring. Right now your self -care is wired to guilt because you are depriving someone of your efforts if you focus on yourself. Let's draw a picture to represent this.

I like drawing to show, but also to help us process things in a way that feels more childlike. Slow and steady is how we do this self- care thing y'all. Now, I know that you might be feeling guilt about feeling guilty. The brain likes to go in circles like that sometimes, so pause my friend. Take a breath. Don't invite any more guilt to this self -care party. You may feel like you should be beyond this, but here you are, ready and willing. Feeling guilty about feeling guilty is not the self-care move you think it is.

Okay, so now let's make some new associations with your care and other people in your life. What if you associated your self- care with helping others more? So if you take a walk outside, then you might discover a new way to help someone solve a problem. If you take a nap for an hour, you will be less irritable and more present with your children. If you don't go out to the event tonight, you can have some time to curate your calendar, and plan something special with your friends for another time. Then our drawing can look like this:

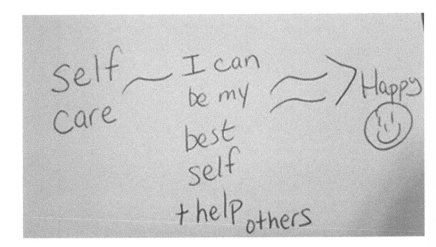

Remember that phrase, 'Turn that frown upside down?' This is what we are doing with guilt. We are turning the guilt upside down by making self- care about adding to, not taking away from in our lives. Should you ever need a reminder keep this quote from author and creative Alex Elle nearby:

'You cannot keep abandoning yourself for the comfort of others and expect to walk in alignment with your purpose. Being anyone but yourself will keep you small and stuck in unhealthy cycles.'[4]

You have a right to flourish. Yes, you.

Have you ever watched someone maintaining a vintage piece of clothing or antique? A lot of time and attention are given to make sure that the item is kept in good condition. It is a painstaking process to ensure that something retains its value. Think about how people fawn over a baby. We use words like precious to describe them because they are precious and valuable. The newness of a life that is just beginning is something we value so much. I know as a mother, when I had each of my children, I did not hesitate to do what I needed to do for my baby because they were top priority.

When does our life become so familiar that we take our own selves for granted? When do we lose this idea that we are precious? You can learn to see yourself as valuable. You can show up for yourself generously. Where do we learn to not take care of ourselves? Did someone say you are not worthy directly? Or do they say it in subtler ways? This answer is different for each person, and is a question worth answering.

---

[4] Elle, Alex [@alex_elle]. Photo of hard truth quote. *Instagram. 16 Apr. 2021, https://www.instagram.com/p/CNu3km7hrXF/*

This can look like people benefitting from your efforts, even if it is detrimental to you. Doing this over and over creates an ecosystem where we have to help others at any cost. As time goes on and we become adults, it gets more suffocating each year to keep up this pace. Your boundaries become negotiable and you practice not having them. As a result, self-care feels near impossible to make time for in our lives. So many people benefit from you drowning, that it makes it hard to save yourself. We practice saying yes to everything. We get used to the energetic load that is helping other people. We get rewarded for choosing anything but ourselves. We get awards for killing ourselves in the name of loyalty, family, etc. No wonder it feels so hard to not feel guilty.

The great thing about practice is that you can practice whatever you want. Now, you can practice associating self-care with positive things that benefit you and those around you. Imagine how you can care for those around you when you are nurtured. The old adage says *you can't pour from an empty cup.* This is partially true because you can pour from a cup that is empty, but do you want to give those small crumbs to those you love? Giving to yourself multiplies to all those around you.

Undoing the guilt and self-care narrative does not change overnight. You have to give yourself time to get oriented to how different it feels to create new patterns with those you love. It can be overwhelming, so start small. Practice saying no to small things, and gradually build up to bigger things that feel scarier. The biggest unknown is how someone will respond. The truth of the matter, is that you can't actually fully predict how someone will respond, and practice will help you lean into how that feels. Remember this about orienting ourselves differently. Similar to when you go from the ground to water, it requires adjustment. It initially feels unsure and shaky until you get your 'sea legs,' and you get a feel for how you will absorb someone's reaction, or the lack of it.

Return often to your picture and image of self- care and joy. Add colors, and add images and symbols that evoke happiness.

Reflect: How will you disconnect your self -care from guilt?

CREATING SPACE

Space. What do you think of when you hear that word? Spaces can be restrictive or expansive. The space we are going to explore is one that is expansive. I love park spaces where people lay out and relax for hours at a time without a care in the world. Having space is about roaming. Practicing self- care is about being comfortable with space that is solely for you to take up. You might have difficulty finding space because you are uncomfortable with the space being just for you. It is natural to repel something that makes us feel afraid or unsure. Creating space for yourself at first might feel awkward as you work through the guilt that we discussed in the last chapter. It might feel like a waste of time. Even when the resistance is there, it is important to keep going. Creating space is the foundational practice for any of your self- care rituals. First, let's create an energetic space that affirms the need for self- care.

- I deserve to be nurtured
- I am valuable

Check in with how it makes you feel to read those statements. Remember naming how we feel is an important form of self- care.

I have to admit when I was new on my self-care journey, I did not treat myself like I was valuable. Let me share a quick story about how I came to understand how I valued myself, when I found myself in downtown Chicago with cold feet in the snow. I had been needing to buy myself some new shoes for months. The pair I had was from a discount store, and I had bought them about a year ago. Living in the big city and commuting everywhere on bus or train, they had a ton of wear and tear. This caused holes to form in parts of the shoes. During this time, I was having some financial difficulties, but it was turning around due to some new opportunities. By winter, I had the funds to buy some new shoes, even if it was just the same pair from the discount store where I had previously bought my current pair. Week after week rolled past and I never made the effort to purchase the new shoes I really needed.

I was now walking to the bus stop while wet snow fell on top of the snow that had already fallen a day before. As I walked to the bus stop, I tried to avoid puddles of water and slippery ice. I ended up stepping in an unavoidable puddle of water and ice. I quickly felt the water. My socks were soaked. I got on the bus feeling the water squish in between my toes with each heavy step I took. I sat on the bus with freezing feet wondering why I had let things get this bad.

This had been a recurring theme of my life. Overlooking my needs until I just could not overlook them anymore. Whether it was holes in my shoes, or running myself ragged until I got sick or something else, this cycle of burning out in the worst possible way was a constant pattern. I had to take a long and loving look at what beliefs were guiding my actions. Why wasn't I making room in my calendar? Why wasn't I using finances and energy to pour into and invest in myself? What badge of honor did I think I was wearing by not taking care of something like getting new shoes? And if I thought this way about shoes, how else was I neglecting myself?

Sometimes neglect becomes a default. We have to notice it, then make a conscious choice to do things differently in our lives. You deserve space to figure things out. Aligning for self- care means doing what you need to do in order to figure out what you need. And honestly that might take a few days or weeks if you have gotten used to silencing your voice. This is why space is so important. It is so critical to find that time to meander, and to allow things that want to bubble up to bubble up. This is time that is not accounted for, time where you just rest easy knowing that what will emerge is something really beautiful. Can you give yourself space? Can you make space for yourself, even if you don't recognize yourself- especially if you are caring for children, and parents, and other responsibilities? If there is a whisper that says yes, then do not ignore it. Follow the whisper of your heart step by step. It will lead you to what you most need. It will lead you to the louder desires that you have turned down. It will lead you to a space where you can see yourself again. I promise that it will be beautiful. It will be lovely. And what will emerge will bring you joy.

FROM ROUTINES TO RITUALS

Your self- care is not another routine on your to do list. Yet this is often how we view our self -care. When I ask busy people if they are practicing self- care, they usually respond with eye rolls and loud sighs. You would think I was asking them to take out the garbage or clean the bathroom, based on their reaction. How do we rethink self- care so it does not feel that way?

After having my first child, I began to find communities that supported my journey to wellness. I had been following one wellness practitioner, Akua Auset, for quite some time. She was a local health and beauty guru who had done makeup for celebrities, and had a holistic approach to beauty and wellness. When she offered me the chance to work with her, I immediately took her up on her offer. I took an online class, which was more like an experience with her. I am not sure what I thought the class was going to be about, but everything she did seemed magical and wonderful. We met weekly online and convened on Sunday evening to plan for the week ahead. Essentially, she was encouraging us to plan our week with more intention. Instead of asking what tasks needed to get done, she asked how we wanted to feel for the upcoming week. When we tried to be vague she lovingly encouraged us to be clear. Once we got clear about that feeling, we created task lists that would reflect that feeling goal. She repeatedly asked us to consider how we wanted to feel for the week, and who we wanted to be.

She asked us to consider our week as sacred spaces. She often talked about ritual. She never called them routines, because she wanted us to change our perspective. It is easy to brush off a task or routine, but a ritual has more weight and meaning. I remember when she introduced the daily rituals that she completed in the morning. Instead of listing things on a board or paper, she made these beautiful, printable cards, which included things like drinking water, stretching, affirmations, and movement. She encouraged us to get beautiful things to remind us of these important rituals. I bought a small glass pitcher to pour water, and I cleared a space in my room to have my journaling time. It was about creating a space that felt how I wanted to feel, and about doing rituals as a way of affirming that desire. It was a reminder to center my wellbeing on what I wanted to be, and not on my tasks. This was about taking care of myself because that was the work, not because it would help me do something else. Taking care of myself was important work.

As you start to develop a self- care practice, remember that it is not about creating another list of tasks to check off the list. It is about thinking about yourself in a way that is benevolent and generous. This is about treating yourself with love and tenderness. This is how you go from routine to ritual.

If you aren't convinced that this change in word matters, let's dive into what both of these words mean. The Oxford Dictionary definition of routine is : 'performed as part of a regular procedure rather than for a special reason,' and 'a sequence of actions regularly followed; a fixed program.'[5] I don't know about you, but that definition sounds boring, like running errands that you don't really like, or taking out the garbage. You have to do it, but it is not because you want to do it. The definition even reminds us that routines are not for a special reason. Words have meaning, and it is easy to see how thinking of our self- care as a routine actually leads us further from the reality of doing it, rather than encouraging us to do it.

Let's look at the word 'ritual.' The first two definitions of ritual according to Oxford Dictionary are, 'a religious or solemn ceremony consisting of a series of actions performed according to a prescribed order,' and 'a series of actions or type of behavior regularly and invariably followed by someone.'[6] At first glance you might not feel like self- care is important enough to be called a ceremony, but let's reframe it. What if taking care of yourself is the most important work you are here to do? What if cultivating yourself is the greatest contribution you can make to the world? Caring for yourself is less about a list of tasks that have no special purpose, and more about creating space where you can reconnect with what is

---

[5] "routine." /www.lexico.com. Lexico, 2021.Web. 27. September 2021.
[6] "ritual." /www.lexico.com. Lexico, 2021.Web. 28. September 2021.

true. A space where you can convene with your spirit and really see yourself. Think about a ritual you have observed. There is something beautifully painstaking about the process. I remember in church when we would take communion. The ushers would carefully arrange the gold platters with small cups of grape juice and crackers to pass out to the congregation. I especially loved this ritual since you got to eat in the middle of what was often, a long church service. I also loved the care and attention that was given to making sure the ritual was done correctly. There was music and the pastor said a few words to bring back the importance of the ritual to our remembrance. The ushers with gloved hands would pass the tray. I waited in anticipation to get the tray and carefully take the cracker piece and the small plastic cup of grape juice. After everyone received their juice and crackers, we all collectively ate the bread and drank the juice. In a few seconds it was over, but it was a moment of reflection and silence that made the ritual memorable.

Imagine if you treated yourself like that. Imagine if you created a life that affirmed how exquisite you are. This is not about expensive items either. There is a difference between luxury and ritual. This is about the way you posture yourself doing certain activities and tasks. Some of the most profound rituals are very simple in instruction and materials. Sitting still and breathing. Watching performers get ready for a show to start. The silent prayer an athlete gives before the biggest competition of their life. Pouring water from a beautiful pitcher. The rituals and opportunities to do them are really endless.

Here are some routines that you might consider shifting into rituals:

- **Waking up:** How do you wake up in the morning? Do you wake up naturally? What greets you as you wake? Might this be an area where you could incorporate some special elements to invite you into the day with more peace and balance? A few practices to consider include waking up to your favorite song; aromatherapy; stretching; or turning off email notifications for the first hour in the morning.

- **Eating meals:** Many times, you might skip meals, or eat quickly because your schedule is hectic. Self-care could be slowing down and enjoying your food. Food has so many tastes. It is important to sit down long enough to enjoy them. Consider adding utensils and plates that will invite you to slow down when you eat.

- **Breaks at work:** Most people do not take breaks at work, even though they are allotted in their schedule. Taking breaks at work is vital and can easily be viewed as a ritual. Breaks don't have to be spent scrolling on the phone or checking emails. They can be spent doing things that bring joy for small amounts of time.

- **Bedtime.** How do you show up to sleep? Are you doing a million things before you go to bed? Do you have rituals that let you know it is time to get to bed? Are there special things in your room that invite sleep and peaceful rest into your dwelling? Some of my favorite bedtime routines include light reading, sitting quietly, putting my phone on do no disturb, and spraying my pillows with lavender.

- **Sleep:** Maintaining a good quality of sleep is a ritual, too. Things you do to make sure you enjoy your sleep from the blankets you use to music to diffusers. This does not just include sleep at night and could include taking naps during the day.

You have a lot of routines that with a minor tweak, they can be crafted into rituals that make you feel good. An easy place you can start is with the morning routine. You can take five things that you really want to do in the morning and write them on pretty paper or cardstock. Ideally each thing can be done for short amounts of time if your schedule is super busy. Think 2-5 minutes. Of course if you have more time, you can lengthen the ritual. After creating those beautiful cards, place them in a container or basket. Every morning when you wake up, pull out a card, then complete as many as you have time to do that day. Choosing them from the basket also offers an element of surprise since you won't be doing them in the same order each day. Some of my rituals include: drinking water, stretching, affirmations, gratitude, and journaling. It is really up to you what you do, and you are free to change them whenever you want. For instance, I had a few months where I would read a fiction book in the morning instead of waiting to do it later in the day.

Whatever you do, remember that rituals are about lavishing on yourself. We know how to deprive ourselves, but lavishing takes some practice. Rituals give you an opportunity to give to yourself continually. Ritual reminds you to show up for yourself differently than you have done before. It is an invitation to take time to set intentions that speak to you living your best life. Giving to yourself with intention can shift how you do everything in life, and the way in which you teach people to engage with you.

Reflect

- Notice. What are you currently doing as a routine? How does it make you feel to do ____? Just write down short phrases without judgement.
- How do you want to feel when you do _____?
- How will you make ____ routine a ritual in your life? Start with one small action and commit to it for the next seven days. Document how you feel each day. Keep it simple.

A note about keeping your action simple

We often want to do all the things mentioned/we can. I know this because I am that person. The key here, though, is to do things that refresh and relax, rather than overwhelm you. Once you start with one thing you can then add to it, but really focus on just one action that you can turn into a ritual. What is one thing that could shift how you feel? Instead of trying to tackle your entire morning routine, you could focus on eating breakfast or hydrating when you wake up or showering slowly. The possibilities are endless, but make sure to take it one step at a time.

It is important to create rituals that fit your current life, instead of what you want your life to be. When we try to create rituals around how we want our life to be, it can be difficult to do consistently. When I had my second child, I didn't have twenty to thirty minutes in the morning to journal like I had done the months before he arrived. Normally, I would have tried to put some unrealistic expectation on myself to get that done, but that would have made me feel miserable. Being more connected to how I wanted to feel gave me permission to do things in a way that made sense for my life. Knowing I was limited on time since I was nursing a newborn, my husband bought me the five-minute gratitude journal. It was a practice that took two minutes in the morning, then two minutes in the evening. I would follow prompts to share gratitude, priorities for the day, and affirmations. It reminded me of what was important, and that made me feel good. Instead of fighting the flow of life, I went with it and found things that worked for me where I was at. You have to meet yourself where you are. It is okay to take small steps. It is okay to modify a self- care practice to fit where you are.

Love the time you have even when that time is limited. If you are struggling with where to start, then begin with being present with yourself for a few minutes per day. Sit down, and just notice of how you are feeling, and what you are doing in a moment.

If you have no idea what rituals would make you feel sacred or special, remember that the process of returning back to yourself takes a long time. It can take a while to know what you really want, especially in an age where you are constantly bombarded with information about so many topics.

If you have been suppressing your desires, you can feel like your life is one big motion that you struggle to get through on any given day. Going through the motions can be a default setting on your life, and the lens through which you see everything including your self- care practice. When you just go through the motions, you don't feel particularly bad, but you don't feel deeply good either. It is a middle ground that allows you to experience life, but not as fully as you know you really want to experience it. You can go through the motions for so long that you start to actually believe that is what you want. But remember to keep listening to that faint flicker in your heart. Keep stoking those embers. Keep making space to figure out what you want. Acknowledging what you really want is the richest form of self- care that exists. Living a life that you intentionally craft can't help but nurture you. A fulfilled life is more than dull motions and routines. It is much more vivid and radiant. Find your way back to that radiance. Step by step. Day by day. Keep going.

Each day you will find that your picture will get brighter and more vivid, as if you are adjusting settings on a screen. You almost won't know that it is happening until you find yourself thinking about something from your past or responding differently to a situation than you would normally have done. You find your way back to alignment faster. That is what ritual does.

Whenever I am languishing and knee deep in worry, I do two things: (i)Play Faith's Hymn by Beautiful Chorus, and (ii) I start writing my thoughts. We often meet ourselves in tough situations. It is in the struggle that you understand, that being still is the one way you actually save yourself. It feels hard to reconcile that when all you want to do is protect yourself, and perhaps save yourself. But ritual asks you to look at everything with new eyes, fresh eyes, graceful eyes. Rituals give grace.

New Orleans is one of my favorite places, probably because it is filled with so much ritual--rituals and traditions are the fabric of the city itself, a rich quilt of culture, history, and heritage. There is much to learn and know when in New Orleans. It is as if things call you forward and you have to listen. I was at a conference in New Orleans for a non -profit that I worked for, and we had planned excursions based on themes. Our group theme was religion, and we visited various places of faith during the day. The heat was sweltering and hit me like a suffocating blanket every time we stepped off of the bus with its freezing cold air conditioning. We found ourselves in front of a mosque to learn about the Muslim tradition and their community work done in the prison system. The first thing we had to do was to take off our shoes and cover our hair. I had been to temples before where shoes had to come off, but not to places where I had to cover my hair. One of the students on the trip with us was Muslim, and she carefully tended to everyone as we tried to make sure we had our hair covered properly. She came to me and gently placed the fabric over my head, before tying it loosely so it covered my head and rested gently on the top of my thick locks. We went into the mosque and had a powerful interfaith panel with leaders from various faith communities in the area who talked about how connected different religious traditions were. For the remainder of the day I felt calm, centered, and at peace. The practice of physically getting ready to enter the mosque and learning about a faith tradition I was not raised in was deeply nourishing for me. That is the power of ritual. The ability to take simple gestures and fill them with a specialness because it feels right.

Myliek Teele, the founder of Curlbox, talks very candidly about her wellness and self- care journey. She reminds us that self -care can look like a lot of different things. As I write, this one thing she is focused on is steaming her pajamas and creating a laundry room that is sustainable and brings joy. At first glance someone might write that off as chores, but she openly reveals that doing these tasks with love and care have a profound impact on her and her internal state. She provides a great example of learning to be curious and then choosing rituals based on what we want, even if it does not seem like the typical thing to choose.[7]

May your return to ritual be a pathway to your self -care that you hadn't imagined before. May you approach your life with a reverence and gratitude that brings you joy and causes you to weep at the same time. May you honor your life and give yourself flowers right now. May living be a delicious

---

[7] Teele, Myliek [@myleik]. *Instagram. https://www.instagram.com/myleik/*

experiment in uncovering your desires, and holding them with joy and love. Never forget how sacred you are, and how special you are. Each breath you take is a testament to the power that courses through your veins and urges you to live this life beautifully and with a sense of ease.

As you take this self- care journey, I encourage you to find communities of other human beings who will celebrate, and hold space for you, as you embrace a life of ritual. It will keep you accountable to what you said, and will also provide support when you find yourself spinning your wheels in routines that no longer serve you.

BEING CURIOUS

Getting my hair done is a form of self- care. When I am not taking care of myself it is reflected in the state of my hair, which grows quickly. When I go to the hairdresser it is the ultimate ritual-of washing, conditioning, and massaging of my scalp. This is followed by moisturizing the scalp. Then they take the time to re-part my scalp so that each lock has just the right amount of hair and that it is untangled. Then rolling the lock, clipping the lock, and they do that meticulously for about an hour. I then sit under the dryer for another hour. After finishing up, I feel like a brand new person and feel tended to. During that time, I often get good ideas or realizations about something I have had on my mind. This is how I self- care. I used to get anxious about my hair appointments taking so long and would want them to rush the process. I would bring work and take conference calls for work. I thought that this was just a necessary thing I needed that was getting in the way of my life. Curiosity asked me to think about this process differently. Every time I came from getting my hair done I felt calm and more connected. When I decided to be present during my time, I reaped the benefit. I began to see that valuing this as time for myself made all the difference. I gave my schedule more space to accommodate the appointment and didn't bring work with me.

Curiosity can help you see things differently. What is curiosity? Curiosity is defined as a strong desire to know or learn something. Curiosity is a healthy inquiry into how something works. Curiosity often involves asking questions, and then asking more refined questions until you get clear about what you are want to know and explore. It is an endless quest to know something deeply. Oddly enough, we also describe curiosity with negativity using such phrases as 'curiosity killed the cat.' How many times have we interacted with a curious child and felt overwhelmed and slightly irritated? Why do they have so many questions we wonder? Because there is so much to know about so many things. There is a pulse to being curious about why the world works the way it does.

Our lives require this same sort of curiosity. You require space and time to get to know who you are, and who you are not. Have you ever wondered why certain things make you tick? Or why do you engage in the same habits time and time again? Have you been curious about the times when you feel completely at ease with yourself and what is contributing to that joy? Or do you shame yourself for not being at a certain point, or not getting something quicker?

Curiosity gives us the courage to savor our lives right now. Savoring life is about savoring all of the parts of you. I remember listening to an Instagram sermon with Pastor Lyvonne Briggs, and she said that we need to love our shadow parts, -you know, the parts that people don't want to see or think about too much. With a curious eye we can examine who we are without judgement. We can feel what is without shame. And if we do experience judgement and shame, we can dive deeper into why we are experiencing that, and where that belief and narrative was inputted in us. Sometimes life requires a loving examination instead of quick solutions. This loving examination can get us closer to a self- care practice that feels just right.

I write this as someone who has struggled with this a lot. I often want to bypass the pain of growth in favor of vain and misplaced solutions that actually do not work. Curiosity implores us to see things differently by taking a good look at ourselves.

Curiosity also has health benefits, too. Studies have linked curiosity to increased levels of empathy, positive emotions, and better patient-doctor relationships. Making curiosity a part of your self- care practices can help you find solutions that are best suited for your unique life situation. Curiosity can offer us a way of leaning into our unique way of being in the world without shame.

Reflect

- How can you be more curious in your life?

Consider adding these curiosity focused exercises into your self- care toolbox:

- **Ask why.** As you are observing the world around you, ask why as if you were a young child. Why is that cup blue? Why am I feeling this way when my phone rings? Why does the GPS not work in certain downtown areas? You don't have to answer the question, but it does get you practicing asking why.

- **Examine what is not working.** Ask yourself what is not working in my life? What practice, system, or routine isn't getting me the intended result? You know something is not working when you are not feeling the desired state from the activity, or not getting the desired outcome. I used to think that I wanted to learn a new language. I would pick up language books and programs from the library and really struggle to do it. It was hard to learn a new language, but it was just so boring to me. Contrast this with when I went to a song-writing conference for the day and it was exhilarating. I had to ask why didn't I like learning the language, or why was it so boring? And the answer was simple: you just don't want to do it. It is something you think you should do, but not something that you really want to do. It is okay for you to change. It is okay for your preferences to be different than what they were last week. You are ever changing and your self- care should be reflective of this too.
- Other questions to ask yourself:

What has piqued my interest lately?
What do I no longer enjoy doing?
Who do I no longer enjoy being around?
Am I feeling how I want to feel when I do____?

Understanding Your Personality

You might be curious about your personality. While these assessments and methods are not a sure thing, they can be a powerful tool for you to understand how you process or interact with other people. This is not an exhaustive list. Take what feels right and move on from anything that doesn't.

- **Human Design.** Human design is like one- part zodiac, but also another part noticing patterns of people. It was helpful for me to understand that I am a manifestor, and how that affects my ability to implement rather than be a visionary.
- **Personality Tests:** like Myers Briggs, DISC, and Enneagrams are scientific and research backed. They are great ways to help us understand personality, and how it affects all parts of your life.
- **Astrology and Tarot.** This is not for everyone, but there might be something to this planetary alignment thing, and how it affects the world around us, as well as how we view the world.
- **Ayurvedic Dosha:** I studied with the Chopra Center and the idea of Doshas, or element types is fascinating. It really reveals a lot about how we can balance the elements within ourselves.
- **Ask a friend.** Asking those close to us to share observations they have about us is another way to unearth information about ourselves, and is a quick, surprising way to get information too.

SELF -CARE HISTORY

A lot of times we are looking outside of our life experience in search of self- care practices when they are right in front of us. As we continue being curious, we are going to explore your self -care history. Documenting our lives is an important practice. Documents, scrapbooks, historical documents are proof that something happened. It offers proof that someone existed in a particular way. I admire people who do scrapbooking and are committed to documenting their life, and the lives of their families with precision. I think of the family historians who painstakingly create family trees for reunions, and those who create beautiful pictures of a family's lineage and history. We do things like this because preserving memory is important. It is especially important when you are creating memories that are new, and will hopefully become tradition over time once you enter the ancestral realm.

How do we document self- care? We can go to some great people for this. From scrapbookers, to photographers, to videographers. They offer approaches for us to think about documenting our lives, and the lives of those who came before us. I think about, 'In Our Mother's Gardens,' a must watch documentary by Shantrelle P. Lewis. She brilliantly and beautifully documents the complex, yet challenging legacies of Black women.

She explores what mothers leave behind, and how that influences how we think about ourselves. She had a section of the documentary about radical self-care that was especially powerful. I think about how we must sit at the feet of our family and our ancestors to learn, and also to make visible the ways in which self- care has lived in previous generations.

For women of color, Black Women specifically, we know that self- care has been linked to survival. How else could our foremothers have endured all of the stress and pain that comes with living in a society that had false narratives about our existence? How else could they have endured a long history of oppression and violence? How do we think about self-care that is not just rooted in survival, but also rooted in us thriving, too?

We often hear the following quote from Audre Lorde: "Caring for myself is not self-indulgence. It is self-preservation, and that is an act of political warfare."[8] I used to read that over and over again. The words spoke to me, but I could not quite grasp the magnitude of it. How could caring for myself be an act of political warfare? It took some living for me to find myself in her words.

When I care for myself, I listen to what I need. As I get used to acknowledging what I need, I begin to come face to face with my desires. These desires are not what anyone else, any structure, any institution says that I want. I think

[8] Lorde, Audre. *A Burst of Light and Other Essays*. Ixia Press, 2017. Print.

of Naomi Osaka risking being fined when she was struggling with mental health during the French open. Or Nikole Hannah Jones, or anyone else who is saying no so they can say yes to themselves and greater alignment. Even in the midst of backlash, and the shock that people feel when we don't value the same thing, you stand strong because you are rooted and grounded. That 'groundedness' comes from spending quality times with ourselves. When we are not obsessed with being number one, or having the most money, or having the most things, something beautiful emerges. This knowing, though, shifts how we view the world and our place in it. It is also quite literally putting systems on their butt because we are showing up different. We are coming in different. This is the movement. It is disruptive to the status quo. Self- care is part of a bigger ecosystem.

And what do you do with movements? You document them so there is witness of what happened. And what existed, and what was, and what really is. Self- care documentation can be simple. I remember watching a Facebook event hosted by Girls Trek at the start of the pandemic featuring Angela Davis and Nikki Giovanni. Angela Davis asked, 'How can we enjoy what we are fighting for if we are not well?'[9] She reminded us that self- care mattered because you have to be alive and well enough to be able to experience the things that you fought so hard for. That is so important. And that kind of self- care has to be self-sustaining. It cannot be a random bubble bath, or some candles or a vacation every six months. There is too

---

[9] Girl Trek. Angela Davis and Nikki Giovanni Live with Girl Trek. *Facebook, 8 May 2020, https://www.facebook.com/watch/live/?ref=watch_permalink&v=549964385668765*

much at stake not to be well. But we also have to know it and share it, so it illuminates things for other people in our lives, and in our history. This is why we document.

I encourage you to take your time going through this chapter. Get the supplies you need to create a rich self- care history for your family. As you answer the questions, find pictures, documents, and other documents to add to the self- care history. Draw your own pictures.

Exploring Childhood: Yourself

As a child, what self- care did you engage in that you possibly didn't realize was self- care? There are no wrong answers. Go with what first comes to mind, and follow the clues. For me, self- care as a child looked like going to the library; sitting on the floor and listening to an entire record while reading album notes; taking baths with Avon bubbles - because it was the premier bubble bath in the nineties; looking out of my window and just thinking about things and imagining; sitting in my closet and reading books. I also used to love to grill food. The process of heating the charcoal; preparing the meat, and cooking over fire became a ritual for me.

Exploring Childhood: Family Members and Friends

Next, think about your close family members and friends when you were growing up. What kind of self-care did they engage in that you can remember? Write, draw, and process these self- care memories in as much detail as you would like.

Did you see self- care modeled around you during childhood? When I first answered this question, I said, "no." I was thinking and envisioning self- care as a series of actions that I had basically seen marketed to me. I saw my mother do some things like taking baths and exercising, but initially, I couldn't think of anything beyond that.

But then I asked the question again with a twist: Did I see people around me doing self- care but just didn't know it at the time? This question has become a part of my reflection. Alice Walker, writes in her book, 'In Search of Our Mother's Garden, '*And so our mothers and grandmothers have, more often than not anonymously, handed on the creative spark, the seed of the flower they themselves never hoped to see: or like a sealed letter they could not plainly read.*'[10]

What secrets did they leave us in plain sight? For me, this yielded so much more for me to draw from. Things like:

- My mother napping during the day
- My mother taking me and my brother to the library each week to choose more books to read, and the feeling I immediately felt when I entered into that quiet portal.
- My father meticulously cleaning the cars and focusing his energy on that task.
- My grandmother sitting on the porch.
- Gardening.
- When my father would be in the kitchen making banana pudding.
- My mother and her sisters jumping double Dutch at family functions.

---

[10] Walker, Alice. *In Search of Our Mothers' Gardens.* Mariner Books, 2003. Print.

And I began to see that I had a rich self- care history that I could draw from if I view it from that perspective. So much joy lives in my self- care history that I wasn't noticing at first.

I remember going to the hairdresser with my mother. This hairdresser's salon was not a stand- alone business. It operated out of the basement of her home. It was a long ride into the city, but the hairdresser did my mother's hair so well, that she didn't mind making the trip into the city, usually with me and my brother in tow while my father worked. We would go into her basement and head into a small room that had been outfitted with a rinse bowl, mirrors with bright lights, counters full of supplies and curling irons, and a dryer chair. It was a mini salon. My mom would get in the chair, while I read my book and waited, since I usually got my hair done, too. She would start talking to Ms. Norrine, and it seemed like she was going through her own process of coming back to herself. This was social and physical self- care. From scrubbing the scalp, to washing the hair, and from blow drying to flat ironing and styling. It was a process that was long, but it was always with much talking and laughing. I don't quite remember what they talked about for those hours, but I do know how my mom felt as a result. It wasn't just her hair being done. It was also her feeling seen and heard after a long day of work. She felt cared for and nurtured. There was magic in that. It is something that I appreciate now going to get my own hair done. It is these memories that often give us clues for how we can return back to self –care or offer us ways that we might reconsider our self- care practices.

Exploring Your Senses

Your senses are pathways into memories, too. Think about smells, textures, and tastes that bring you joyful memories. These memories may lay a foundation for self- care practices that you design for yourself. When cooking, I get a bit of joy from cooking rice. My grandma made the best rice. She made a pot almost every day for my grandfather's breakfast. Every time I make a pot, I think of her. I sweeten it like she did, and when I eat it, I imagine I am sitting at the kitchen table in front of the AC unit that was right next to the table blowing cold air. I would love to be at her house and to see her doing that each day. Keep a running list of all of these things, as we will return back to them when we talk about play.

Exploring Childhood: Inquiry

After you recall memories, ask for more details with family members who would be open to share and elaborate on how certain things made them feel. We often can get more information when we hear the stories from other people. Questions like: What were you thinking about when you were on the porch? Why did you garden? How did you learn to bake? How did you feel when you listened to that album? These questions can be illuminating, not just for learning about the people we love, but also as a way of showing the rich tapestry that is caring for oneself, and the ecosystem that we often think was invisible, but was very vibrant and present.

Present Day Self -Care

The next part of the self -care history is focused on your self- care practices as an adult. This is like taking pictures and thank God for social media where we can share them. Look back in your feed and pull out the experiences that were really nurturing for you; wherever it was self -care just how you wanted. You might, as I did, find some experiences where you did it because you thought you should. Don't include those. Really choose the ones that you know and felt were self- care. For me, making a new recipe with no expectation or time pressure; reading fiction; starting my pandemic garden; organizing my oils and spices; attending a concert with my best friend; bowling with besties; Michelle's earrings; attending a Broadway musical; traveling; tea and crepes at the spot; slowly eating macaroons.

And then you know I am going to ask: Why? What made the experience so nourishing? Answering that will highlight so much. Thinking of tea and crepe time, what made it so nourishing? It was time by myself. It involved all my senses -from the taste of the tea and crepes; to the smell of the tea; and visually pouring and sipping the tea; the touch of the warm tea; to music playing that was calming. It indulged all five senses, and that is so important in feeling balanced.

Another memory for me is reading fiction. I love sitting somewhere reading a good book. I feel transported to a new place, and it activates my imagination. It allows my mind to explore without being distracted by other things. This self-care is about focusing on something that is not attached to my adult responsibilities.

Some other memories to consider as you document your own self- care journey:

- Times when you had a great time with friends. Was it a place, the group of people, and/or the experience itself?
- Are there places that bring you to a point of stillness, like a museum, or a faith based venue?

Future Self Care

The last part of documenting is for future generations. This process is not about if you have children or not. Your legacy is larger than blood lineage. Think about the people in history who have influenced us and are not directly related. Someone may read your words or know about how you lived, and that could influence how they decide to live. This is about future casting and giving a context for what you hope self-care could be, and look like for the communities and tribes you care most about.

Some prompts to get you going:

- What do you want to be the norm as it relates to wellness, self- care, or mental health?
- What would be your quote, proverb, or saying that people would remember about self -care?
- What do you hope self- care looks like in the future? What hopes do you have for those who will come after you?

Enjoy your time documenting your self- care history. It is such a rich space to draw from. As you continue to read this book, visit your self -care history often for inspiration, and to add new memories that emerge, too.

Reflect:

What surprised you about doing your self- care history?

What practices will you incorporate into your self -care practices?

SELF-CARE AND LISTENING

As you immerse yourself in your self- care story, you may realize that there were things you completely overlooked about yourself and those around you. You may also notice gaps, though, in the experience that you and others close to you had. Sometimes we don't know what creative self -care or any other type looks like, because we have not seen anyone else close to us do it. In these times, it is important to observe, and then find our own pathway.

People often say it is hard to be what you cannot see. When we see someone else doing something that we want to do, or something we had not yet imagined, it is empowering. Sometimes you cannot imagine or envision self- care for yourself, because you don't actually know what it is supposed to look, feel, or sound like. When this happens, we default to traditional ideas like bubble baths and candles. We have to find others to inspire us to create self- care practices that are substantive and freeing.

Through my work, I connect with people from different identity groups, but a lot of my work is centered on how self -care shows up for Black women. When I write parts specifically about black women, though, I do hope you still read on even if you don't identify as a black woman. Doing so increases your empathy and offers a way for you to be an ally to Black women in your network who are carrying so much on their shoulders.

When I think of black women in a historical context, we have toiled for everything we have gotten. For every fight. For every opportunity. For every achievement. Many of us have seen our mothers toil, both mentally and physically. There is a chance that we have not seen self-care as being something we can afford to do given our responsibilities. This narrative still persists, because even when we get access to more money, more resources, more time to actually do the things, we still may not engage in self-care. I have seen this on so many of my virtual retreats with black women who are entrepreneurs, lawyers, doctors, and so on. Often we need models for what this self-care journey could look like in real life. The frequency of seeing these instances matters. It isn't enough to just see one other black woman doing it, or one diverse character on a show. We need to see more because our experience is nuanced. This is why it is so important to listen to others instead of comparing. This is about really listening deeply to ourselves and our histories for clues that can lead us to self-care practices that feel just right.

There is room to grow and analyze and imagine. And that is the beauty of social media. Oftentimes we are mimicking because we don't know. So we take the trips and we buy the items and we think that if we just do what they do then we will get the peace, relaxation, and love we desire. But mimicking leaves little time for listening sometimes.

Sometimes you have to listen to yourself. Just listen with no pretense. Sometimes you imitate learning by thinking about how we play instruments, or cook, or doing anything else. We have to imitate in order to understand the basics, in order to figure out this new thing we are doing. Or in order to wrap our mind around developing a new skill. So many times in my work people will say, " Kandice, what do you do for self- care?" I might say that I color, or take breaks . Then I notice that they do it, too. That is a start, but then they want something more, which they usually don't meet with curiosity. All types of stories come up about it, maybe procrastination or self- sabotage. I don't think it's those things. Sometimes you just aren't feeling something because it isn't totally yours. There comes a time, when you have to put your own unique spin on your self- care practices.

Putting your own seasoning on something makes it yours. It is why no apple pie is the same, though the same ingredients are being used in some variation. I love seeing this happen in dance competitions. A participant initially learns the choreography carefully, and they practice repeatedly. Then it becomes so second nature that they can then put their own style on it. Once it is time to perform they are doing the given choreography, but with their own unique way of moving to create something really beautiful. Our self- care practices demand that same consistency and experimentation from us. We keep practicing and find what works until it feels right for us.

You have to do your own unique thing for self- care. This book and other resources are a start, but it's not the complete story for you. You have to slow down and keep listening, then take action from that place of desire and knowing. It means making mistakes. It means showing up. It means imitating, but then trusting that you can figure the rest out.

Bubble baths may not be what you like. You may not want to color another coloring book. You may not want to take walks outside or meditate. And you know what? That is okay. You get to change your mind. You get to try new things and new methods. In a little bit, we will talk about how play can help you try new things. That is how you reimagine your self -care. By asking questions and listening, you will find the answers that you seek. Through your own wisdom, through your self- care history and through the inner wisdom that is yours, you will come to know and understand life through a perspective that is more expansive than you may have originally imagined. Your self- care practices are a wonderful way to experiment with creativity, with imagination, and with your life. They become testing grounds for the bigger, riskier things you want to do. When desires start to come up, just let them be. Don't try to explain them away or overthink them. Just let them live there.

I was journaling today, and it was really focused on examining what was not working in a loving way. And all of a sudden, I thought about architecture. I simply wrote it down and let it live somewhere. I then asked my husband why don't we go on an architecture tour. He was game and told me that it would be interesting. We haven't planned anything, but it feels good to let a desire just live free without trying to over-think it or create a long plan. Meandering with our desires is the place where we really get to know them, and listen to the messages they are trying to give to us.

PART 3: RESTORE

CREATIVE SELF CARE

truly believe that creative self- care is the most overlooked type of self- care. Picking up the book, The Artist's Way, by Julia Cameron[11] has been one of the most pivotal parts of my self- care journey. When I first got the highly recommended book, I had no idea that creativity would become a part of my self- care routine. I picked up the book because I was feeling stuck in my writing and wanted to move past the block. I had been working on a fiction novel and found myself wallowing in adding anything new to it. The Artist's Way promised to be a solution to a common problem of stuck creatives. I do not know what I thought the book was going to be about, but I definitely didn't expect anything that the author suggested. I was actually a bit skeptical at first. Much of how she framed creativity was about the spiritual nature of this energy that we all possessed. The first chapter was about mindset and affirmations. The subsequent chapters and activities were really about finding the root cause of creative blocks, usually criticism from childhood, or the critique of a well- meaning (or not so well-meaning) teacher. And the weekly activities were focused on confronting all of those

---

[11] Cameron, Julia. *The Artist's Way: A Spiritual Path to Higher Creativity.* New York: J.P. Tarcher/Putnam, 2002.

things that had us running scared to create the things that we most wanted to create.

The one main component of the method was going on an artist's date. This date was an activity that was fun and child-like. In The Artist's Way, the author explains that our inner artist is really our childlike self. To get it out of hiding, we have to do childlike things, instead of berating it so that we could cultivate and really appreciate our creativity. I started going on these weekly artist dates, which felt so awkward at first. It was trips to the candy store, finger painting, and swinging at the park. These short dates were really great to do and I found myself even looking forward to them a little bit. I didn't always see how they would help me be creative, but I think that was the point.

As humans, especially adult humans, we want to know how things are connected. Input then output, which is a very factory model way of doing things. We want some kind of guarantee on the actions that we take. We want an exact return on our investment. This kind of one track thinking prevents us from seeing how seemingly unrelated things are actually very connected. This causes us to neglect creative self- care, when it is one of the most important types of self-care for us to include in our everyday lives.

Let's think about the powerful energy that is creativity. Creativity allows us to take ideas and turn them into reality. It allows us to find many uses for one thing. It provides us with energy to express new ideas and things never before seen. Everything around us, from our bed to our book, to our computer, was the result of a creative mind having an idea.

And like so many skills we want to learn them, practice them, and get better at them. Normally we go to school and learn and take tests to show competency. Creativity doesn't work exactly like that. Creativity requires us to play and entertain new ideas in order to be cultivated. The things that creativity requires often feel like a waste of time to our adult ideas of learning and growth.

For me, it was because I couldn't get a grade, or get some assurance of being proficient. Trying to measure my creativity on some sort of scale caused me to overlook the results of me playing. When I played, I felt calmer and I was more productive. I didn't see it that way at that moment, but when I looked at my output I realized that this was happening. I was writing more. I was releasing stuck emotions. I was creating and seeing the world with new eyes. These methods were working, even if it did not seem like it was at first.

Creative self- care will stretch you because you can't see the outcome in your logical brain. You can feel the positive effects, and you have to trust that instead of a more rigid way of thinking. Creative self- care really does encompass so many other aspects of self- care. In order to dive into my creativity, I had to pause and rest long enough to hear myself. Daydreaming is the stuff that creativity is made out of, and it requires doing something opposite to the daily grind we find ourselves in. It taps on our emotions, spirit, and social patterns.

Remember, you are a creative being. Creativity is not just relegated to a chosen few who sell best -selling albums, or write best- selling books, or star blockbuster movies, or have amazing TED talks. You have creativity and you use it often. If you don't feel creative that is okay. You are often using your creativity in service of someone else. That someone might be your children or your spouse. It could be your employer, or your church or civic organization. Our creativity is usually on display in those kinds of mutually collaborative situations. No wonder it feels hard to tap into creativity when we detach it from the outcome of being responsible for someone else.

So, how do we find our way back to our creative selves? We play. Seriously, we do things that bring us joy. Things that turn off that part of our brain that is so critical and full of judgement. You can start really small--go for a walk; collect some shells, color or draw, finger paint. Basically act like a young child. Look out the window and daydream. Do these for a few minutes to get used to listening to the childlike wonder that is always speaking to you. You don't have to believe in the positive effects of play in order to do it. You might be skeptical, create anyway. The name of the game is to have fun anyway, even when things don't feel productive. Your inner artist does not like to focus on being productive, which is so boring. This is where play comes into the picture.

Permission to Play

In school playgrounds all over the world, you can hear kids screaming and running in organized chaos, managing not to bump into each other for the most part. Laughter and feet on pavement is a constant backdrop. The children never stop moving, even as sweat starts to moisten their faces. Whenever it is time for recess, children impatiently wait for doors to open so they can run free. When the door opens, or when they let go of an adult's hand, they know exactly what to do.

If you lean in closer, you realize that recess is an entire ecosystem where an entire range of activities are happening simultaneously. Some kids are running around in circles. Others are playing an organized game with roles and imaginary worlds. Some kids are squatting down looking at something on the ground, perhaps watching a bug crawl past them. Others are reading a book. There is another group talking to each other. Some are using chalk to draw. Sometimes there is a playground where children are convening. Other times, there is not. Many children, especially those in urban areas, play on sidewalks or parking lots. It doesn't matter, though, because children know how to do recess no matter the physical location. During this time children let out all of the energy, their vibrancy, and their joy. After being cooped up in classrooms all day, this is the time to do what you want with very few rules to limit your time.

I always wonder why society, particularly in the United States, limits play time for children, especially as they get older. By adulthood, play feels frivolous and like a waste of time, though we can see the joyful effects it has on children. Oftentimes, adults want to limit it for children, too. Almost like we don't want to be reminded of just how much fun it is. It kind of reminds me of the Grinch who stole Christmas, but this is the Grinch who stole recess. Sometimes I fall into that category. If I interviewed my five –year- old daughter she would tell you that I often am the bearer of bad news at the park, telling her to pack up so we can go home. After all, how long can you really run around for? According to my daughter, "forever." Play seems to suspend any sense of time, and us adults are here to reinforce that time because we have to get back to the other things we need to do, the serious things.

What if we lived our life with pockets of play? What if we allowed ourselves the time to carelessly do what we wanted with no expectations? What if we gave ourselves permission to play just like those children now as adults? You may not be fully convinced. After all, we are adults now, and we have too many things to do. And those too many things do not include playing. Let's reconsider that when we think about creating a life that centers our self- care.

Play is powerful. We know this from a few different perspectives. Our personal experience with play is our first window. Many of us can recall times playing at school, at home, or at family gatherings. We can remember screaming, yelling, feeling like time passed by so fast when we were playing outside or indoors. Remember how an hour felt like five minutes, and when it was time to be done it felt so hard because you could have run around forever?

Our second window into play centers around observation. If you have children or have been around children for any period of time, you have observed them playing. While it may initially look like children are running around aimlessly or playing games that make no sense, there is a method to the madness. During play time children are negotiating boundaries, engaging in competitive activities, learning new things, and understanding how to socialize with their peers. On the playground you learn how to successfully or unsuccessfully deal with conflict resolution; develop spatial awareness, and conquer your fears.

Our third window is research. There is so much research on play and it suggests that it is more beneficial than simply letting children burn off some energy. Children who get more time to play do better academically. Play can be a powerful way to help students develop social emotional skills, as they learn to notice and regulate their emotions. Research also shows that the effects of play don't magically stop when we are children. Play has benefits for adults, too. Many of the effects are the same as for children. Engaging in play can increase productivity, make us more creative, and be a tool to manage our mental health. From this vantage point, play is a very important part of self- care. If we know this, then why don't we see adults running around or playing more in public? Where are the large gatherings to promote play? Why are we not doing this thing that is so important for our physical and mental health?

We are often socialized to do the exact opposite of play, so much so that playing as adults can feel awkward and embarrassing. 'Adulting' is serious business. We have a lot to take care of and responsibilities to manage in this very busy life we are living. If we are being honest, play does not seem like the best use of that time does it? What is the end goal of this play time? We start asking that question and see the answer reflected in how we design secondary education. We stop getting recess in high school, and much of that physical activity is reserved for sports, or the cafeteria, or goofing off in the classroom. Many activities that we liked to play have become about competition, scores, and scholarships, which isn't much fun. No wonder we avoid playing as we move into adulthood.

I am not going to tell you to go to the park or do something that feels embarrassing. Though, I will tell you that embarrassment quickly subsides once you are actually doing something like swinging, running around, or playing tag. The wonderful thing about play is that you can infuse it in so many different ways into your life that do not take much time, or many resources to start it. Remember the benefits of including play in your self -care practice-increased productivity, cultivating creativity, and positive effects on mental health. You might feel silly, but silly is sometimes just what you need to unwind from this so-called adult life that can feel all too rigid.

Story time! One of my first consulting gigs was with the teaching program that I had trained at to become a teacher. I was tasked with rebuilding their mentoring program, and creating programming to build an inclusive community amongst the diverse teaching candidates. The teaching program was a rigorous program -requiring a year- long teaching residency in a school, compared to the usual eight-week student teaching most schools required. Teaching candidates were stressed as they prepared for a stressful career.

I was developing an activity that would build community during orientation week for the new teacher candidates, and hopefully to give them some important take aways. I wracked my brain trying to think of something, and I thought about the students they would be teaching. Shifting to that, I immediately recalled field day at my school. When I was in elementary school we had Field Day, which was an ultra-competitive day where families were involved. The school was split into five or six teams labeled by color. Parents were also encouraged to participate. Shirts were ordered, and on field day you wore your colored shirt. There were games all day and scores were tallied to see which team would prevail. You really didn't know who would win because there were activities happening everywhere and there were all types of races and games that would determine the winners and losers. The winner usually got some little cheap trophy, but the bragging rights were the ultimate prize. I remember how much I looked forward to those days, and it was so much fun to play the games. So in roaming around my memory bank, I decided that we would organize a field day for the teaching candidates.

Next, I knew I had to pitch the idea to the staff...and I didn't quite know how it was going to go. After all, they were professors and Ph.Ds. who were experts in education, literacy, and research. Would they actually go for this idea? I pitched them the idea, with the caveat that play was beneficial, it would give them an experiential way to really understand the power of play, and it would also give teacher candidates the opportunity to blow off some steam and learn how to relieve the stress that would inevitably come with teaching. They loved the idea and we planned for the day.

We used the field across from the building where we had class, and set up stations and games just like an old school field day. We hired a gym teacher from a nearby school to facilitate the field day. For two hours we played. We did potato sack races and relays. We did all sorts of games and played tag. Everyone came in for lunch out of breath and ready to reflect. We reflected on how to disagree and how to be supportive of others. There was a lot of laughing, and many people said that it reduced their stress. It was a powerful experience that informed my work.

I become even more obsessed with play, diving into The Artist's Way, by Julia Cameron, which had become my go to creativity book. I learned just how important play was to creativity. In the book, Julia Cameron explains that our creativity is very much linked to our child self.[12] When we interact with ourselves like a child, we actually cultivate more creativity in our adult lives. The process of becoming unstuck as an artist involved going on artist dates, which were essentially play dates. I committed to the process and took those dates doing everything from coloring, to going on swings, to collecting rocks. Each time I do the program, I am amazed at just how important it is to take the artist's dates.

Remember that our definition of self- care is something that energizes and restores you. Play is a powerful tool for our self- care journey if we give ourselves permission to play. There is so much we don't know about play, because we don't allow ourselves to do it as adults.

The first thing is to create a play history which was coined by doctor and play expert Stuart Brown. In a play history, you think about yourself and what you liked to do at certain ages. You can group it in clusters of years,

---

[12] Cameron, Julia. *The Artist's Way: A Spiritual Path to Higher Creativity*. New York: J.P. Tarcher/Putnam, 2002.

or from younger child to-older child. Or simply make a list. Think about all the things you used to love to do and play as a child; everything from games to toys. Also think about things that you enjoyed to eat or do that were not necessarily play. These things become great ways to compliment your play experience. Yes, you will be playing, but more on that later.

Spend some time just going back and thinking of all the things you loved as a child. As you start thinking of things, more will come, but give yourself time.

> *What was your favorite color?*
> *What music did you love listening to?*
> *What cartoons did you watch?*

Once you have this list, it can be a great roadmap for how you can incorporate play into your self- care routines. Play can run the gamut of all types of self- care--so it is important to try things out and see how it makes you feel, because that really is what matters with self- care. Looking at your play history, let's do something fun called self- care mash up.

Self -Care Mash Up

Take a piece of paper and make two boxes. In one box, write the things that you do for self- care right now--let's say baking; napping; and doing yoga. In the other box, write three things that you loved to do when you were a child -let's take coloring; watching cartoons, and building forts with blankets. Now take one thing from each box and create a new self- care activity for yourself. Using my example list, here are some options for me:

- Baking cartoon cookies
- Building a nap fort and taking a nap in it

Reflect

- What will you do more playfully in your self -care practice?

EVERYDAY EXTRAORDINARY

We often talk about mindfulness in these boring terms about staying present, but mindfulness is simply noticing what is happening around you. This practice can be playful and a way to bring joy into our lives with ease. Your life is one large classroom, and your life experiences are your greatest teachers. I am not just referring to the big life moments like having a child, or being in a relationship. I am also talking about the everyday, often overlooked, moments. The ones that are subtle, yet so powerful. Like observing a dog playing in the grass, or watching a child laugh, or feeling raindrops on your face. It is the act of **noticing** how rich your current life is and exploring how that richness can lead you to more joy. Your life is extraordinary right now.

One of the first pieces of advice I give to people in my workshops is to pause and notice the world. There is much to learn from noticing. Simply noticing what life is trying to tell us. Simply looking at the mile markers that the universe is laying out. Being still long enough to get the exact wisdom that we need at this exact time. That is what everyday extraordinary is all about: pausing, noticing, reflecting, and being guided by life.

How do you practice everyday extraordinary? It's simple. Stop and notice what is happening around you. Then, ask yourself "What is this teaching me?" and gently allow an answer to present itself.

It's that simple.

You are wise. You have what you need to live a life that reflects your truth. Allow your experiences to guide you on the journey.

I wanted to share a few of my favorite everyday extraordinary moments with you as an example of how the smallest things end up being the most amazing mindful moments.

Trust the Process

My two-year-old daughter takes ballet every week. A dance class made up entirely of two-year-olds is CHAOS. Most of the time, my daughter, Inara, rolls on the floor or hops around the room, completely ignoring her teacher, Ms. Robin. Ms. Robin goes over the dance no matter how the children are acting. The routine doesn't change, and she reminds the little dancers to plie, then passé over and over again. She reassures all the parents that this is a part of the process, and that showing up consistently does work. **Let's just say I had my doubts.**

While I was making dinner a few days ago, I said, "Plie," just like Ms. Robin does in class. Imagine my surprise when Inara actually did it, and did it correctly! Turns out she was listening to Ms. Robin. She even did a passé, too. I was in shock, and Inara was beaming proudly.

Isn't life like this, too? We get into a new routine. We begin learning something new. Maybe we start working with a mentor or a coach, and it seems like none of it is working at first, then, all of sudden things start to click. We know more than we thought we knew, and we start to make lots of progress. You absorb way more than you thought. So keep going, my friend, keep going. **Trust the process. Keep showing up. Watch the magic unfold. Surprise yourself.**

Where do you need to learn to trust the process in your life?

Heartbeat Good

One night my daughter came up to me and asked, "Check your heartbeat?" I nodded my head, and she proceeded to gently touch my chest. She looked at me and said, "Heartbeat is good. Heartbeat is good."

I had a lot on my mind that evening, and that simple statement returned me to the present. It was a gentle reminder that my heartbeat is right here and right now. A reminder to pause and be grateful. A reminder that I am blessed to have a heart that is beating and supporting my life. When everything in life feels wrong, I know that my heartbeat and breath is good.

Find peace in the present. Stay in gratitude for the life coursing through your veins. Remember that you are alive with potential and hope every single day.

Put your hand over your heart. What do you feel deep within you as your heart beats?

Blessings on a Cold Day

I was driving on the expressway with my daughter one day. The temperature had hit the teens and the heat was cranking. As I excited a ramp, the check engine light started to flash, and the car struggled to maintain speed. I pulled over onto the shoulder, and turned the car off. I turned the key in the ignition, and the car wouldn't start, and I even tried again with no luck.

I called my husband, and he said he would catch an Uber to our location. It would take about an hour for him to get there since it was rush hour. I was concerned about the car getting cold and my husband recommended I call an Uber so I could get home quicker. I ordered an Uber, but I was in a spot that didn't have an exact address. Even though the driver was close, it took about 20 minutes for him to find me. During this time, the car started getting cold. I sat in the back with my daughter trying to keep her warm and calm. The driver called me to reassure me that he would find me.

When the driver finally arrived, he got out of the car and helped me with my bags, as I carried Inara. When I got into the driver's car the heat was on full blast. He turned around and asked, "Is it warm enough? I have had the heat on since you called so it would be nice and warm for the you and the baby." I nodded and expressed my gratitude.

We chatted for the duration of our ride, and he told me he had just left a job interview and was about to return home. Since he was going home, he had decided he wouldn't turn on his Uber. He drove for a few minutes and he felt a nudge to turn it on while driving on the expressway. A few minutes later, my request came through on the phone.

You never know who you might affect when you follow those nudging's within yourself. In my case, it was such a blessing on a cold day, and a reminder that it is always a good time to practice kindness.

How can you be a blessing to someone today?

Reflect

- What everyday extraordinary moments happened in your life this week? What lessons does it teach you in this moment?

EMOTIONAL SELF-CARE

woke up on a Sunday morning and nursed my five- month old. My husband had gotten the vaccine and had been out of it for the past two days. He is a stay-at-home dad, so this meant the kitchen looked like chaos. I decided that I wanted to try a new recipe to use up some over ripe bananas that were sitting on the counter. I had my five- year- old settled watching television, and my five- month old was in his high chair playing with a crunchy book that he could bite. The only thing getting in the way of me and my banana muffin recipe was this messy kitchen. I had most of the items I needed, but a few items were dirty. If I am being honest, I love to start cooking in a clean kitchen. It feels disjointed to clean in a kitchen that is in disarray. So, I cleaned up the dishes and cleared the counters. I knew my husband would get to it eventually, but I wanted those banana muffins, now.

I began washing the dishes, and immediately started to feel irritated. Now usually, I would let the irritation heat up to a boil then explode on everyone around me. This time, I just noticed what was happening. As I started to feel the irritation, I felt my demeanor shifting. My I daughter started asking me lots of and my reaction to her was short and snippy. Then,

I started to key in on the clutter in our living room followed by the bags of garbage that had not been taken out yet. It was like this feeling was affecting everything I was seeing.

This kind of moment is when emotional self -care is needed. I got curious about what I was feeling. Internally, I asked, "What are you feeling?" It was clear I was feeling irritated. Further interrogation actually surprised me. I thought my irritation was solely with my husband, and his less than consistent kitchen cleaning schedule. I simply asked why I felt irritated. And you know a nagging voice came up that said, 'Adulting is an everyday endeavor, even on the weekends.' Then what came up was the amount of responsibility I had when I was younger. I was the oldest child, so I was often responsible for making sure my brother did his homework and came home on time from playing outside. In addition to my studies, I often made dinner and cleaned up the house to make things easier for my parents, who both worked and had a long commute.

I remained curious about the source of this irritation, which was coming from past things, yet was affecting me now. While I could talk to my husband about doing dishes in a timely manner, the bigger issue was being tired of doing chores. This was something my teenage self totally felt often. I imagined that my younger teenage self was voicing her frustration and I approached her with love. I took a moment to comfort her, just like I do with my daughter when she is having a hard time. I told myself, "You know, this is hard. It is hard that you have to be an adult all the time. It sucks sometimes, too because on the weekend you just want to do nothing. Yet sometimes dishes need to be washed, and sometimes your children need things, and that is hard stuff sometimes."

As that happened, I felt my irritation subside. It turns out that, that emotional self -care was just what I needed. I was able to deal with the dish scenario with a different energy. Whether I talk to my husband about remembering to do the dishes, or consider hiring housekeepers to come an additional day, or if I decide that I am not doing dishes on weekends, and we will just have to use plastic or paper plates; this is coming from a responsive place and not a reactive one. I also realized that I needed some alone time that didn't involve work, which meant I needed to make some space for me to do something for myself that felt restorative.

Learning to respond to emotions, and the things that trigger those emotions, requires learning how to tend to your emotions in a consistent way, so that they are constructive rather than destructive. Some of my favorite ways to do emotional self- care are:

- Journaling
- Trying new scripts with communicating and internal conversations
- Therapy
- Meditating
- Using the feelings wheel

These methods give me time to sort through the murky territory of feelings. Emotional self- care has helped me to identify that I can be emotionally reactive. Emotional reactivity is 'the tendency to experience frequent and intense emotional arousal'.[13] Many of us have not been taught to deal with or acknowledge our emotions. In an attempt to deal with the strong arousal, we often do impulsive, regrettable things if we are not aware of what is going on. Emotions are energy, and that can be strong energy that we do not know how to diffuse. I am grateful that we have mental health professionals who help us to understand ourselves in a deeper way, so that we can live more balanced lives. Emotions need to be honored not suppressed. And suppressing emotions does not actually stop them from running the show, or from triggering things in you.

Emotional self- care is probably one of the most important types of self- care, because it can literally affect the other areas of your life, including making you physically sick. So much of how we view the world is through the lens of our emotions. So much of our emotions are rooted in, or attached to stories and experiences from our childhood, particularly our early childhood.

As you practice emotional self -care, you will become more aware of how your emotions, and subsequent thoughts, are affecting how you act in the physical world. That is a big deal when you learn to stop yourself and do something differently. As you dive into emotional self- care, make sure to take good care of your physical body. It can be overwhelming as you sort out your emotions and process memories and experiences, and also to deal with shifting relationships, but

---

[13] Karrass, Jan et al. "Relation of emotional reactivity and regulation to childhood stuttering." *Journal of communication disorders* vol. 39,6 (2006): 402-23. doi:10.1016/j.jcomdis.2005.12.004

freedom is on the other side. And that freedom includes not feeling guilty about taking care of yourself, not being overwhelmed by the stories that others tell, and learning how to respond to the world in a healthier way than you had been taught.

You are making choices everyday. Choose to heal. Know that you deserve to heal. You deserve tenderness and care. When someone comes back from surgery, they are tended to by nurses and medical staff to ensure they recover properly. That recovery usually requires lots of rest, hydration, and customized care with medicine and other medical interventions. The same goes for your self- care. As you uncover and heal wounds, be gentle with what you are becoming. It is okay to grieve the comfort you used to have that is no longer there. It is okay to not feel okay. It is okay to not want to be positive for positivity's sake.

Start simple when you begin focusing on emotional self-care. One place to begin is by simply naming your feelings and observing how they make your body feel. You might notice that anger makes your skin feel hot. Or nervousness makes your stomach feel queasy. You might notice how your heart beats faster when you are worried about something, or the way your shoulders tense up when you feel irritated. Focus on naming your feelings. If you, like me, are not sure how to do this, then get a feelings wheel template from a reputable online source or a therapist. It is a great tool that gives you a basic set of feelings (happy, mad, sad) and then gives you more specific words that are associated with those core feelings. So I might be feeling mad, and then from there

I realize that I am feeling frustrated. Also, the feelings wheel keeps us in our power. When I was studying for my Chopra health certificate, one core component of living a balanced life was emotional freedom. So much of how we express our emotions is disempowering. We want to blame someone rather than own what we feel. There is no one universal way to react to something, and we have to own up to that. Emotions are often layered, meaning the original trigger usually is compounded by past experiences, which have shaped how we view ourselves and others.

When you start to recommit to your self-care practices, you might feel restless. It can be hard to slow down after going so fast for so long. It can also be difficult to orient yourself to slowing down once you start doing it. Practicing self-care requires patience with yourself. We often move so quickly through life that we don't realize how impatient we are with our own progress. And oftentimes this happens automatically, so we don't quite understand it until we are moving at a different pace.

Self-care brings us back to this question: who am I when I am not doing all of the things I normally do? Who am I when I am not exhausted? Who am I when I am not putting everyone else's needs above my own? Who am I when I am not measuring my progress by all that I have done? Who am I when I tap into who I am being? These are not easy questions to ask, and at certain times they are even harder to answer. Yet, the answering is where you find yourself again, where you find freedom again, and where you notice just how wise you already are.

Restlessness is energy that you have to move through. You cannot bypass it. You will continue to be restless until you do the things that you truly desire, until you truly come and meet yourself face to face for what you truly are. That restlessness and churning is often a signal and message that you are ignoring your desires -the thing that you overthink yourself out of because its frivolous, or out of reach, or not in line with your perfect vision for yourself. Or the thing you try to complicate so much that you end up putting it back on the shelf to let it collect dust.

You don't even entertain how you might make it happen. I simply asked you to show up and do your part. Not my part, your part. Your purpose is bigger than what you can imagine. It is bigger than your selfish plans. It is bigger than your limitations. And it is much bigger than your fears. This is why you surrender. This is why you accept. This is essentially why you rest.

You are a channel, and that can feel hard because you have to simultaneously bring the work to life while also surrendering to the flow that is coming. It is a delicate balance to be an active participant and a conscious bystander. So much of birth is like that, there is so much that is not in your control; how the sperm meets the egg and turns into a child; how the embryo grows... you are simply carrying a process that is unfolding and happening without your input. At the same time, you experience symptoms of this process and you have to do things like take vitamins, rest, and eat so that the process can happen.

Surrender and acceptance. Surrendering is not passive. You have to be intentional as you also allow life to happen. So it is with your purpose. You usher it in and bring it forth by doing the work -writing, dancing, resting, singing, and expressing your gifts, but the seeds that come to fruition are not up to you. You have to stop spinning your wheels on stuff you cannot actually control. And when it comes time to birth something, you find out once again that you oscillate from active participant to active bystander because eventually you surrender to the process. You are no longer in control, and you are no longer pushing because your body is pushing for you. It is happening without or without you, but how often do we not even get to that moment because we prematurely cut off life to this growing gift, seed, or fetus that was entrusted in our care? Rest is the requirement. Self- care is bigger than you and me. It is transformational.

I have only felt super drawn to two things--teaching, or guiding, and writing to uplift and inspire. Seriously, my greatest work has included those things, yet that is the thing I avoid doing the most. Somehow my ego has convinced me that being busy rather than being diligent is the answer, but it is not. I know no time is wasted, yet I convince myself that it is too late, but it is not. I am breathing. Therefore, it is not too late. The bigger question is can you wait for the right time for the right idea, for the right moment? That is the real question.

Can you rest instead of being restless? Can you write instead of being restless? Can you teach instead of being restless? Can you guide instead of being restless? At any moment you and I are exactly where we are supposed to be. With that awareness I am never missing my moment or missing the alignment or missing the opportunity. Ever.

SHIFTING SELF -CARE RITUALS

Your self- care rituals won't stay the same indefinitely. Whenever someone comes to me who practices self- care, yet feels stuck or tired, I check in with two things: boredom and familiarity. Getting stuck in a rut is normal with anything from work, to schedule, to eating the same food. Being familiar will also make us feel like we are in a rut. Sometimes, we have to spice things up, just like with a marriage or a friendship we have had forever. Self- care practices are exactly the same. It is important to periodically check in with yourself and make changes and adjustments to your self -care routines so that they can continue to be restorative for you. Here are some things to consider when you are thinking about shifting your self- care practices.

When I was in fifth grade, I was so excited to start playing the flute. I walked quickly towards the band room for my first group lesson. I assembled the flute, and was instructed to blow air across the lip plate. The other students squeaked out a sound, but nothing for me. I tried again and no sound. It ended up taking me about four weeks to get one sound out of that flute. During that time, nine- year- old me wanted to quit. Yet, my music teacher told me to keep practicing. She told me to keep trying and to continue positioning my fingers as if sound was coming out.

Showing up to practice each day was just as important as what I actually did during practice. Even if I'd had a not so great day, it mattered that I showed up and stuck with the process. Over time, I eventually got a note out and grew tremendously as a flute player.

While we understand the importance of practice as adults, it can feel more difficult to embrace in real life. After all, we have bills to pay, endless to do lists, and so many people who need us. The idea of practice can be overwhelming as we try to incorporate new routines into our lives. No wonder it can feel so hard to create new habits, which can take 18-254 days to form[14]! It is no different with self- care. Making space for self-care is a practice. We have to commit to caring for ourselves, which often bumps up against what we were taught; our internal beliefs, our current schedule, and other's expectations of us.

I remember when I listened to a beginner meditation video and the instructor said, *'If your mind wanders during the meditation, gently bring your awareness back to your breath. Don't try to make yourself stay focused perfectly. Just guide yourself back.'* They did a motion with their hand that mimicked that action. That felt so simple to me and relieving. It wasn't any pressure to have to stay the course perfectly

Rather, the practice was to bring my awareness back to my breathing and the present moment. Of course, over time

---

14   Lally, P., van Jaarsveld, C.H.M., Potts, H.W.W. and Wardle, J. (2010), How are habits formed: Modelling habit formation in the real world. Eur. J. Soc. Psychol., 40: 998-1009. https://doi.org/10.1002/ejsp.674

your mind becomes accustomed to it and it feels natural, but it takes time to get there. Instead of focusing on how hard it is, we just have to bring ourselves back to the practice of being in that moment.

Self- care also requires this same type of patience. You could be on a consistent schedule with your self -care rituals, then suddenly stop doing it for a host of reasons. Instead of beating yourself up, and then probably not re-engaging with your self- care, you can bring yourself back.

Instead of getting bogged down about why you haven't been doing it, just be aware. Then, do something that makes sense with the time you have. My therapist encouraged me to do this, and it was successful. Instead of over-thinking about why I couldn't stick with my self- care ritual, she said to first just do the self- care thing, which in my case was to take a bath that I had been skipping out on. Once I was actively engaging in the activity, then I could reflect on why I was having difficulty being consistent. It was much easier to reflect since I was doing something calming and relaxing, and the key was to bring myself back to what I most wanted.

Taking care of yourself is a practice. There are so many messages that tell you otherwise, so it takes real focus to have a consistent, self- care practice. If you have grown accustomed to not seeing you as a priority, it can take time to learn new beliefs about how you view yourself and your care. It may take a while for it to feel normal to practice self- care without guilt. Even when you get off track, you can always bring yourself back. The returning back is the practice. When you notice that you have neglected your self- care remember a few things:

- Awareness is a gift. *Celebrate that moment when you pause and acknowledge something isn't* feeling quite right for you. This is a more graceful approach than criticizing yourself for getting to this point.
- *Ask yourself:* What can you do in this moment? How can you make your self -care a priority in this moment? Small steps matter my friend. It might be taking a breath, or stretching, or reading a funny joke...
- Once you bring yourself back, then re-affirm your commitment to your self- care. Put reminders in your phone or calendar for the remainder of the week for your self- care practices. Or have a close friend hold you accountable.

Your self- care practice is an ongoing, ever-changing thing. Give yourself grace as you learn how to make it a regular part of your routine.

Before and after major life changes are often times when we need to adjust our self- care practices. I experienced this while being pregnant and giving birth during the pandemic to my second child. My self- care practices were about quick, impactful times like the gratitude journal that I would do for five minutes. I also became more committed to resting and napping because I was so exhausted. Additionally, I had to create more boundaries with family during this time in order to manage my energy during such a stressful time. During major life changes, such as divorce, marriage, pregnancy, worldwide crisis, and moving, all require a good amount of energy and shift so many things. During the pandemic we found this out in real time just how stressful it was to navigate things changing so much. When I think back to all of the change it is kind of bewildering. From a new baby, to pivoting my business, to moving to a new home, and the death of my husband's grandmother, it was a lot of changes that really could have overwhelmed me. If you are experiencing some major changes, take some time to pause and shift your self-care practices and check in with your current needs, which probably are changing more rapidly than usual as you navigate the changes happening in your life. Here are some other changes that will have an influence on your self- care practices:

- **Seasons.** One of the core beliefs of the Ayurvedic tradition, which is focused on finding balance through engaging all five senses, is understanding how to find balance between your internal and external state. Practices such as meditation and breath work, as well as mindful eating are part of Vedic traditions. One thing that is very important in Vedic traditions, is following the cycles and movement of nature to stay in balance. Each season is focused on a certain element and depending on your personality and mind-body constitution, you could get out of balance depending on the season. For some, the heat of summer is a comfortable reprieve from the colder months. I know I love sweating and feeling the sun on my skin being absorbed. For others like my husband who is a fiery personality, the heat can be unbearable and get him out of balance. Look to the seasons and think about how you might need to shift your self- care rituals as result.

- **Menstrual cycle.** I remember many years ago my friend, Fenesha, told me about how much she was learning about menstrual cycles, and how they affect our day to day living. Each week of the cycle, (because your period is not your cycle), women can feel different according to hormonal shifts. She told me use my phone to to track my menstrual cycle and plan my life around certain weeks in my cycle. Instead of pushing through social events during week four, (the week that we all know as PMS week), I didn't plan anything and stayed home to rest and read. During super social times, I planned things during week two, when the hormone goddesses were in my favor. Knowing how your cycle works can be a game changer in knowing what type of self- care you might need, and how you might need to shift things based on what week you are in. Do a search about your cycle, and then start observing how many days each phase lasts for you. It really is a practice in noticing yourself and then honoring what is, rather than beating yourself up for not working at 'optimal' capacity all the time. Optimal capacity is when you hit your stride and know what and when to do that, with all that is happening and part of you. Instead of working against or around your natural flow, you really learn to work with it so that it is less stressful for you. The key here is to be accepting about our bodily functions and how we do things. Unfortunately, society has not been focused on women or our daily and weekly patterns. This can be a powerful window into honoring your body and understanding what types of self-care practices you need at certain times.

- **Age.** You are not the same person you were when you were twenty years old. Heck, you are not the same person you were yesterday. Sometimes, time makes us different...not just because of major life events, but because of the business of living. This living alters our perspective, matures and grows us, and even challenges us on what we thought was the norm. It is important that our self-care reflects these changes. Perhaps a self-care ritual like yoga was beneficial in your thirties, but now as you enter your fifties you find that you need something more energizing like dancing to get you going. Or you might find that a few years ago you used to love reading fiction books, but now you are really into watching documentaries. Changes happen as you change. Also, as we get older we often get clearer about what we really want. Some of us may have been hiding because of how we thought we needed to be perceived by important people in our lives. It is okay to have changing preferences and priorities for your self-care. That is normal, and it shows that you are a healthy human being. Allow yourself the gift of changing, and honor that fiercely, and be grateful for what is on the horizon as you learn what kind of self- care works for you in the future.

It is okay to try something new. It's okay to return to something else. Sometimes you have to take it all apart and rebuild it again. Know that you can switch your self- care practice whenever necessary.

Your Personal Retreat

When you are shifting your self- care practices, it is important to pause long enough to really understand what you need to shift. I like to call this my personal retreat. The great thing is that you don't need to spend any money to make this happen. This process is also how I plan my signature virtual retreats, too. The process works, and it feels easy to do, so let's get into planning your personal retreat. I recommend doing this at least twice a year.

Getting Ready

Set the date and put it in your calendar. Plan for at least 60-90 minutes, and make it an appointment in your calendar that no one can disturb. This is the most important part. What you value, those around you will value. Ask for help. Delegate tasks. Create this space. And take your time making sure this can actually happen. The biggest part of self- care is actually planning it into your busy schedule.

Get your playlist ready. Create a playlist with your favorite songs that bring you relaxation and joy to set the mood for your retreat. Most of the streaming services also have great curated playlists for certain moods, so be sure to check those out. Music is always a great backdrop, and can get us in the mindset of nurturing ourselves. Treat this retreat like a special event, because it truly is. You are the event. Act accordingly.

Get snacks and beverages ready. Get your favorite healthy and nurturing snacks and beverages ready for your retreat time. Maybe cut up some fruit or make a charcuterie board. Or you might just like a glass of water. Get whatever is refreshing to you. Remember, this is a main event. I love getting yummy fruit, seeds, and tea. Sometimes a fancy bottle of sparkling water is what is on the menu.

Getting Centered

Start your retreat getting centered. This is about focusing your mind and remembering to be present. Being present is the first form of self- care. Some things you can do:

Breathing: Take a series of deep breaths. You can do traditional breathing (inhale through your nose, exhale through your mouth or nose). Or you can try techniques like box breathing where you inhale for four counts, hold the breath for four counts, then exhale fully for four counts.

Tip: as you breathe, make sure to relax your shoulders.

Grounding: Notice a few things in your environment. I like to do 5-4-3-2-1. Five things I can see; four things I can touch, three things I can hear, two things I can smell, and one thing I can taste. I also like to do color grounding, which is to find as many objects as you can in 10 seconds that are green. Then switch to another color.

How does it feel being centered?

Making Space

What you do next is really up to you. It is all about doing activities you enjoy that make you feel good. Choose three or four activities to do as part of your retreat experience. Choose from the following, or come up with some ideas of your own:

- Choose a window from around the world on the Window Swap[15] site and journal
- Read poetry, quotes, or excerpts from texts about self-care, joy, etc.
- Look at images and reflect on what they mean to you. There are so many accounts online to do this. Some of my favorite places to get pictures are from Kenesha Sneed, and the Gordon Parks Foundation.
- Take a walk outside
- Do yoga
- Dance around the room
- Take a nap
- Paint
- Garden
- Play Dough

---

[15] *WindowSwap*, https://www.window-swap.com/.

- Coloring books
- Try a new recipe

Reflecting

After spending time doing your retreat, do some reflection. This can be as simple as sitting comfortably on your couch and thinking about a particular question. Here are a few questions:

What type of self-care am I needing most right now?

What have I been neglecting about my self-care?

What about my self-care is not working?

How do I want my self-care practice to feel?

Closing the Retreat

- Express gratitude for having taken the time to re-center yourself.
- Commit to adding more time into your self-care rituals each day. Also commit to shifting your self-care rituals if that is what you learned during your reflection time.
- Do a ritual to symbolically represent closing the retreat. This might be lighting a candle, doing a chant, or listening to a song.

One last thing to remember is to be patient with yourself. Practicing anything takes time and it can be frustrating. Though we don't want self-care to be like that, it is. We have spent a long time not honoring our desires, and a lot of time not prioritizing our wellbeing. So it feels awkward at first, but saying something is not working is a big step. Or saying I am not feeling this, or this isn't actually bringing me joy. You may not know what you want to do, but you are one step closer to uncovering it because you know what you do not want. I don't really meditate. I find meditative moments when I am walking outside and what not, but you will not find me on a cushion meditating for thirty minutes. There are so many self -care practices, and finding the routines and rituals that bring you balance is a great adventure.

Children everywhere do this beautifully. The only moment they are in is now, and they deeply feel whatever they need to in the moment be that: excitement, boredom, sadness, or frustration. Then they act accordingly, and find the tools and resources they need. That is how you need to be with figuring out your self- care formula. Just like with any great recipe, it takes time to find the right ratios so that you feel satisfied and nurtured, but it is possible. Once you find it you will honor it, and if you fall off the self- care wagon, that vision will keep you going and bring you back. Self- care all the time is really about finding your way back daily. Finding your way back to what is true for you. Finding your way back to your needs and desires. And finding your way back to the peace and the joy that you really deserve. That message can get lost in the noise of our lives, which is why hosting a retreat for yourself is so beneficial and life bringing.

PART 4: RECLAIM

CURATING THE CALENDAR

When you look at your calendar how do you feel? Does it feel like there is not enough time? Do you feel like you have a wide open space to do what makes you happy? Or maybe you are somewhere in the middle. Your calendar and how you view it can be one of the greatest supports or barriers to creating a sustainable self-care practice.

Is your calendar a buffet or a gourmet meal? Both types of restaurants, a buffet or a fine dining establishment, have good food and have happy customers. The experience is where it differs. At a buffet, you get your pick of a lot of different foods. As food runs out, more food is replaced since you can eat a lot at a buffet with how it is set up. The output from the kitchen is rapid, with dishes having to be made over and over to satisfy the customers. Buffets tend to have a menu that is palatable for a variety of preferences and tastes. Unfortunately, you might not find many dishes that are specially made for certain diets like gluten free or vegan. You might find some items, but the majority of the items will be for the middle of the road tastes and preferences. For this reason, many buffets don't necessarily have a specialty, and can make many things well.

Now, let's shift to a fine dining restaurant, but more specifically a restaurant that is very boutique like ones you might see on Master Chef. At these restaurants, items are usually seasonal (if not changed more often), so the dining experience is always new. Also, because the food is very specialized, the restaurant offers a limited number of reservations. In these places the guests are not going up and getting their own food. Rather, they are given the food in courses that build upon one another. In this way, the chef is under control. As a result of having this very high touch service, the cost is more expensive. The portions at these restaurants are not large because it is about getting the most optimal serving that will showcase the perfect blend of flavors. With more than one course, you do end up getting what you need, but not all at once like the buffet. The chefs are meticulous about knowing their clients' food preferences ahead of time, and take great pains to accommodate special dietary requests.

What does all of this have to do with your calendar? How you view your calendar, and who has control of it is what makes all the difference. Your calendar is a living document, and a mirror into how you feel, and the choices that you are making. It is a mirror into what you prioritize, and also a picture of what you don't find important. When I used to look at my calendar, I felt defeated and sick. Each part of the day was filled with conference calls, appointments, and chores. I remember telling my husband that I felt like I was on a hamster wheel. It just never felt like I had enough time to do all of the things that needed doing, especially things I loved doing like writing. I felt overwhelmed. I knew that something had to change, but I was not sure what to do. I wanted a solution so badly that I overlooked really understanding my calendar, and how it could support me.

Do you view your calendar as a buffet, or a seven-course meal? Who is in control of your time? If you are buffet style, then your calendar is open game. If a spot is open, then it is available. Anyone can come and take what they need. Everything is urgent, and you are always accommodating everyone else's requests, because if you have the time on the calendar then you will allow someone to take it. Just like a buffet model, this requires a lot of output. You are in the kitchen making lots of items all of the time to keep that tray full all the time. But the thing about time is that it starts to run out, and then you find yourself scraping the bottom of the pot or pan trying to give away the last bite. Ever hear anyone say there is never enough time? That person is most likely experiencing time as a buffet. You do get time to replenish, but then it is back to running out because people want more. If you don't have boundaries and do for everyone, of course they enjoy it because it is good for them. Unfortunately, it isn't sustainable for you. Imagine having to make food for a buffet with a small staff. The only way this works effectively is if you have a lot of staff members. Someone who can check that food is getting low, someone else to check on customers, and someone else to make sure that new food is being cooked at the right time so that customers are not waiting for long. The other thing about a buffet is that it becomes hard to focus on one thing, or to prioritize because you are doing too many things.

Now let's think about the boutique restaurant way of doing a calendar. This means that you are in control of your calendar. You determine how much time you have or want to spend, and then from there you give people limited access to you. You are also doing things that are in line with your passion and joy, and are delegating to other people. Each week you are taking into account what is happening for the week, what you really need, and making space for time to brainstorm and create. You do not do everything, but what you do decide to do is special. You are creating an experience that is thoughtful, and that experience changes as your life or the seasons shift. It is very responsive to your needs. And while it might be challenging to execute at times, there is a flow. Also, once you run out you are done, and then you give yourself time to replenish before re-opening. This is curation.

So how do you start to curate your calendar?

1. First realize that your calendar does not have to be a buffet. Just because time is open on your schedule does not mean you need to be available. You have to give yourself permission to reorient how you view open space on the calendar. Repeat after me: "It is okay for there to be wide, open space on the calendar." Wide open space gives you room to figure things out, or to do something unexpected. This goes back to reconnect with how you are currently feeling, and how you actually want to feel. When you really clarify the gap, you can actually build a bridge and do something differently.

2. The next thing is to add breaks into your calendar. Society makes us feel like we have to do everything back to back without any break, but that is not sustainable. Schedule the breaks in a natural way. Schedule meetings for thirty minutes with people, but put thirty-five minutes in your calendar so you have a buffer. If you use a calendar scheduling platform, you can easily add in buffer time in between appointments. This could also look like giving yourself more time after a doctor's appointment, so you are not rushing back for a call. Breaks are an easy experiment in making space when you feel like there is not enough time in your calendar. If you find yourself in a back to back appointment kind of day, learn how to give yourself grace and ask for it. I realized that I had a back to back day with no breaks. I emailed the person who I had scheduled the meeting with and was honest. I wrote, "I need to be five minutes late to the meeting so I can take a quick stretch break before our call." They appreciated me not just showing up late without warning, and they also appreciated me being honest about what I needed. That five minutes was a game changer, allowing me to use the restroom, stretch, and get some water. Breaks in any form are a form of self-care. They are impactful, even if you only have one minute. There are so many studies out about micro-breaks and their benefits when you are working. Breaks give you time to pause. They also give you time to process what you just heard, and to integrate it rather than ignore it. When you are scheduling breaks,

make sure to include varying amounts of time. Every day you should be taking short mini breaks all throughout the day. At least once per day, work up to planning a break for fifteen plus minutes. Also resist the urge to not take your break because you are feeling okay. When doing studies about breaks, researchers noticed that participants didn't fully take their breaks, opting to do light work related tasks instead of taking the full break.[16] As you can imagine, this practice doesn't give the same benefit as a full break. Allow yourself to take a fully break. One way to get the benefits of breaks is to move your body. Moving your body through stretching, dancing, running, walking, etc. is a great way to give your mind a break. The most important part of breaks: joy. Some scientists believe that enjoyment is what make breaks so important.

Is it really urgent?

One morning, I was in the middle of tending to my baby when a call came in from a client. It was at a time when I do not respond to client requests, so I let it go to voicemail so I could focus on my child. Then, she texted. I quickly glanced at the set of texts, and soon assessed that the issue was not urgent.

Since she was working on it right now, she was giving it 'right now' energy. It would have been easy to absorb that 'right now' energy. Honestly, I was often the one doing that, totally shifting what I was doing when I was interrupted by

---

[16] Staffordshire University. "Why do so many of us feel guilty about taking a lunch break?." ScienceDaily. ScienceDaily, 17 June 2020. < www.sciencedaily.com/releases/2020/06/200617121453.htm >

someone needing something from me. This time, though, I closed my eyes and took a deep breath. I chose not to absorb that energy. I checked in with myself and asked if it was urgent to her only, or urgent for me? If it was not urgent enough for me, then I would be brave, and not be sidelined by the request. I continued with the task I was doing, and reminded myself that it was okay not to rush. It was okay not to respond right away to someone who needed something from me. I kept breathing. I finished my task. Then I calmly messaged back, resolving the problem at a time that worked best for me.

Sometimes self-care looks like pausing and choosing not to rush. Notice when you rush to respond to something that does not actually have a deadline, or you feel compelled to reply right away simply because it is in your inbox. Rushing around sometimes is a default way of being, but we can slow down. In the midst of every moment, there is space to breathe. Choose to take your time this week. Leave a message unread for a minute to catch your breath and respond. Set realistic deadlines for your work so you can ease into projects. Treat yourself well and then others will act accordingly. Recognizing what is truly urgent versus navigating urgent energy is a practice in prioritizing, which leads us to the next way to curate the calendar.

3. Remember your calendar is a boutique restaurant. Unlike a buffet, you are only serving a very specific menu. In prioritizing that menu, you know what you need to buy and what does not need to be bought.

Having priorities helps you to know what you need to focus on for the week. There are a ton of tools that offer methods for prioritizing. I borrowed a method from when I was teaching elementary school called, 'Must Do May Do.' You put on the list three things that must get done, and then three things that would be nice to get done. You don't move to the may do list until you complete all of the must do tasks.

Once you define your priorities you will have to say no to things, even good things in order to make your priorities happen. It will disappoint people, but they will be okay. Even if they are not, it is not something you can control anyway. Saying no means, I am saying yes to something else that matters. When we have too much on our plates, we are saying yes to too many things. This is common when we go to a buffet and fill our plates up to the top. Curating our calendar, like fine dining, means that we have to focus on a menu and painstakingly say no to other parts or ingredients that don't fit the recipe we are making for the week or month.

You will disappoint people when you start saying no. If you are a chronic people pleaser or the yes person in your communities, it might feel like you are saying no a million times over. Curating your calendar is about making intentional choices, and about making changes when things are not lined up with that intention. Because I love a good cooking show, we will keep with the reference. Sometimes when a chef is preparing something, they realize they need more salt. That is a simple fix and they can quickly add it. Yet, with some dishes, like in baking, the issue is that too much of something was added. In this case it is much more difficult to correct the problem, and many times you will see a chef discard an item and start over. They will not serve a plate that is not a good representation of that menu. The same goes for your calendar curation. Some days you are going to create the space and have intention. From that vantage point, you will be able to add tasks or events in, or put more effort into what you have scheduled because you got the basic steps down. Other times, though, it won't go like that. You will look at your calendar and it will be full again with no room to breathe, and not honoring your priorities. Instead of pushing through, you will need to discard and rearrange, because the intention matters most. That will feel painstakingly uncomfortable as you cancel meetings or reschedule. You might decide that you need to postpone something, or temper expectations on something else you had planned to do. At the end of that, though, you will have created the dish that you wanted with your week, and that is all that matters. As hard as it is to send back a dish, the chefs still have to correct it. And that is the point about curating your calendar. Just like with everything else in self -care, it is a practice. As adults, we don't often focus on practicing and how frustrating it can be. As children and young adults we are constantly learning new things: we learn how to walk, talk, ride a bike, read, work, etc. And while we do practice in adult life, we become less focused on the act of practicing and more focused on having it together. Yet life is always calling us to practice, and to lean into what is true for us. And funnily enough, we crash and burn, we fall down, we make mistakes. Instead of seeing them as part of the practice process, though, we feel guilty and embarrassed which leads us to try to be perfect rather than learn the lesson of something not going well.

After having my second child, it takes me much longer to get tasks done. It might be because of a pregnancy brain or being sleep deprived. Whatever it is I can't get things done in short spurts and need to plan my calendar accordingly. If I think I can complete a task in one hour, I give myself two hours. We often need more, not less time to get things done.

Block out tasks. Focusing on seeing one task to completion is a form of self- care. This method may be really helpful in how you think about your calendar. You not only prioritize your calendar, but you work on similar things at the same time. Your brain is focused and does not have to shift as often so you actually get into a flow.

Your calendar is the one tool in your control, even if you don't feel like it right now. I remember a colleague of mine wanted to use Fridays and Mondays to write and to spend time with her granddaughter. She could not see how she could make this work because she had so many commitments with her job. This felt overwhelming so we had to break it down into smaller parts. The first thing we did was put holds on her calendar for the times that she did not want to be in meetings. This hold was more energetic at first since her Mondays and Fridays were still pretty packed for that current month, but as we went further out, she could make decisions with this in mind. Also seeing the hold on the calendar was an affirmation of what she wanted to be possible, and that hold looked like a meeting hold. Then, she went through the calendar and saw what meetings she had on those days. We did an assessment and grouped things as either 'could absolutely be rescheduled, might be able to reschedule, or could not rescheduled.' It turns out most things could be rescheduled, which only left a few things for the next month or two that she would have to do during this time. I want to note this was progress. Going from six meetings during this writing time to two or three was huge! And as she stuck with the process, she was able to go down to one meeting, and eventually no meetings. The whole thing was to get started. As she got into a rhythm with her writing and spending time with her granddaughter, she didn't want to fill the calendar up with other things. It is important to give yourself small wins so you are motivated to keep going, especially when it feels hard to disappoint people as you learn to manage your time. As a result of doing this she is writing and getting her book done. She is also having some sweet time with her granddaughter. She occasionally will schedule a meeting during that time, but it is sparse. She also schedules meetings more in advance. Folks can't just get on her calendar with last minute with requests that are not super urgent. She is being more realistic with her clients about what she can actually get done in a certain amount of time, so she can allow for more time for self- care and wellness.

It is possible for your calendar to make you feel joy when you see it. For you to look and say, I hand crafted this calendar. This calendar includes time for me to give myself what I need. I give myself time to get done what needs to be done. If you look at your calendar right now and you feel overwhelmed, take a breath. Examining and investigating is a step. Probably the most important one. As you figure out what your calendar needs to look like to make your wellness sustainable; be patient with the process. Some things take a while to unravel. You might have to ask yourself many times, what is really not working? When do I find that I crash and burn? When has it not felt like this? What was happening to make it feel more spacious?

Some habits take time to shift. Continue asking, 'What is not working?' Use your feelings and what you are doing as data, not as points against yourself. Let me repeat, use your feelings as data. Use your experience as data. You can look at data and then experiment with what to do next. Pouring guilt upon yourself for not doing it, or berating yourself does not actually help you change anything. Here are some 'data points' to consider:

- Does a particular task or activity make you feel drained?
- Are requests from certain groups of people constantly taking up your time (i.e. family, work, social club, etc.)
- Are their chores or errands that take up more time than you expected?
- Are there certain times of the month that you need to give yourself more time to do things (i.e. children starting school; menstrual cycle, end of year audit at work, holidays...)
- And the last question is: Where are the energy leaks in my calendar?

What is an energy leak? Energy leaks are seemingly small tasks that add up very quickly to cause a lot of stress. These are tasks that:

- You think you can do quickly
- That you could delegate or,
- Things that are not the priority for you, but you keep doing.

We often ignore these energy leaks and like a tire, it eventually gets flat at the worst possible time. Think getting sick right before a big event, or feeling totally burnt out right before or during a vacation. Sometimes these leaks are obvious, other times they are not. It is finding the things that seem like they are not. Kind of like a game of 'Where's Waldo'. Where's _____ Energy Leak?

One thing that was an energy leak for me was meal planning dinners each week. I had convinced myself that it was not a big deal. I had even convinced myself that it was fun, until I started getting very irritated every time I was in the kitchen deciding what to cook, or online buying groceries and trying to remember what I needed for some recipe I wanted to try.

I usually did it on Saturday mornings so it didn't feel like a big thing, but it was still slowly taking energy away from me, and causing me to feel anything but joyful, happy, or calm. I had tried some things that worked with regards to grocery shopping. I now only do pick up and order online. That saves me about 45 -60 minutes each week, since I do not need to step foot into a grocery store.

For meal planning, I tried a few things like signing up for a meal prep subscription service and having designated themes for each night like Italian or vegetarian. I also planned meals in a spreadsheet each week to track ingredients. That worked for a while, but when life got busy the last thing I wanted to do was a meal planning spreadsheet, or making sure I kept track of all of the recipe links. Can you see all of the energy links in this one activity? I was just leaking out energy all over the place.

I complained to my husband for the umpteenth time about it during a month when I had too many things to do. He suggested that we eat the same exact meal on certain days and stick to it for a month. For example: Mondays, we eat spaghetti; Tuesdays, we eat chicken and rice; Wednesdays, we eat couscous with veggies, and so on. Then we knew exactly what we had to get from the grocery store, and it was easier to see what needed to be replenished. This meant faster online ordering of groceries and Saturdays were not spent in overwhelm trying to find new recipes each week.

I was hesitant at first. Okay, let me be honest, I was resistant. I started to feel guilty about not having the energy to plan meals, or to come up with new recipes for my family. I told him it was not going to work and moved on to doing something else. Sometimes solutions to our self-care don't come in bright, shiny packages.

I mulled over the idea for about an hour and then had a moment with myself. How I was doing things was not working, so maybe I should entertain something new, even if that meant telling my husband he was right. My pride definitely didn't want to do that, but I needed to figure out how to stop this energy leak. I agreed to try it for the next two weeks. I chose meals that we really enjoyed, and I thought about what made sense for certain days. For example, we always ordered pizza on Fridays as a way to celebrate the end of a week. On Mondays, no one wanted to be in the kitchen at the start of the week, so it was a slow cooker chicken meal that was easy to prep and ready by the time everyone was home and ready to eat. The plan was to change the meals up monthly if we needed some variety. It has made everything faster. Grocery shopping was a breeze because I could re-order my last order, and add any specific new items that we needed. It was easier to delegate who would cook dinner since we knew what was being cooked that day. My husband had his favorite meals to prepare and I had mine. I also asked for help, and if I ordered groceries, my husband would pick them up. During this busy season of life, trying new recipes just was not a priority. We may not keep this schedule forever, but it stopped up some major energy leaks that were happening as a result. It turns out that closing up that leak has given me more energy for other things like playing with the children, resting, and consistency. I have space in my mind, since I am not trying to figure out meals and recipes. I also know what I want to eat. Do not underestimate the small shifts that can actually make the biggest difference in your calendar, and in how you take care of yourself.

I believe there is a way that we can live life that supports us effortlessly. Essentially it is creating life systems, but systems get a bad rap don't they? The word has its own energy, and honestly, the word just does not do it for me. It feels boring. But systems are ways that we can think about life and how it flows. We also do not have to prescribe to anyone's systems either. I look to others for inspiration, but I have to create systems for my life that make sense. I am currently writing this book at four thirty in the morning because of how life is set up with a nursing baby. A year ago, you could not have paid me to wake up at this time, and it would not have been productive for me to get up this early. Times change, and we can either respond to the changes or try to fight them. Guess which way works better? It is being responsive to the changes, and creating systems or modifying life systems to actually help you do life better. And doing life better is self-care. This is the type of self-care that is not about doing one off things like bubble baths or massages. This is about creating an ecosystem that supports you living a life that does not cause you to be overwhelmed and spread thin. It is the basis for creating self-care practices that are consistent and relevant to where you are in your current stage of life.

One definition of system is this: 'A harmonious arrangement or pattern.'[17] What if your calendar was harmonious? What would that look like? Feel like? Sound like? I find that we often don't even let ourselves daydream because we are always in the mode of wondering how it will get done. How can you build a house if you don't get a rendering and blueprint first? What would harmonious look like for your work? For your family? For your personal life?

---

[17] "system." /www.lexico.com. Lexico, 2021.Web. 29. September 2021.

Create a masterpiece with your calendar. May your schedule illuminate the brilliant vision you have for your life. Live a life that is exquisite by creating it one day at a time.

Morning Rituals

Mornings are another chance and another opportunity to try again, to refresh, to regroup. Yet, mornings are rarely seen with this renewed sense of energy. Rather, they are an invitation to an already busy, hectic schedule and a life that leaves us wanting more. What if your mornings were different? What if they inspired you to keep going and moving forward on the things that were most important to you? What if they restored your energy, rather than remind you that you don't have enough of it? What if...?

This chapter is about morning rituals. How to create them, how to use them, (not efficiently, but energetically,) and how to use them as a jumping off point for a continual self- care practice that just keeps getting better and better.

The first crucial part of the morning ritual is understanding where you are, so you can get somewhere different. We often don't know what we are actually doing, and it becomes hard to say what we really want when we can't name what we don't want. My husband would say this is examining and understanding the problem. This is different than criticizing the problem. It is about being an observer of what is happening and simply asking, 'Is this working?' If it isn't working, then you assess why. This is not the time to feel guilty about not doing something. Guilt only keeps us in a loop of our own making, which never materializes the thing that we keep feeling guilty about.

Right now think about your morning routine as it is. What do you do? Really think about how do you wake up? How many times do you press snooze? Do you eat breakfast? Do you check your phone? What are you checking on your phone?

Now on the other side, make a list of how you feel. How do you feel once you are done with your morning routines? Be honest, no shame. When I first did this, I realized that my morning routine made me feel tired, uninspired, and dull. You can go deeper and ask, 'Why do I keep doing things to feel this way? Is it obligation? Or because I don't know anything different?' Or do you need support? Really get curious and write down whatever comes to mind.

Now, think about how you want to feel in the morning. Don't focus on what you would *do*. We often go over to the solution too quickly. Think of three adjectives that would describe how you *feel*. We start with how you feel because it offers more solutions. You might be checking your emails first thing in the morning, which starts to make you feel anxious. You might say stop checking the emails. But that might still make you feel anxious if you are worried about work related matters. So that may not be the real solution. You might need to do affirmations before checking email, or you might need to dance and move your body. Perhaps you might need to put your phone on 'do not disturb' so you are not hearing your emails going off every few seconds. So think about how you want to feel, and start to brainstorm what you could do to make you feel that way. As you do this, simplify what you are doing.

Next, consider examples of things that you might not think of for your morning routine. We often do things simply because we have not seen anyone else doing it, or we make assumptions. Do what works for you! At times, I love to read fiction books in the morning. Sometimes you have to do things that fuel you. Certain activities are not necessarily evening or morning activities.

If you are like me, you have a million things on this new morning list and don't have enough time to complete them. Choose two things on that list that would make a difference in your morning right away. Circle those two things, and focus only on doing those two things for the next two weeks. You might still check emails on your phone, but you will do positive affirmations and also take a walk outside. Focus only on one or two things.

Also, use the time you have. If you ideally want to walk outside for thirty minutes, but you only have ten minutes then use the ten minutes. The all or nothing thinking is not going to get us to gradually create self- care practices that matter. We often get into all or nothing because of guilt -thinking we have to do something fully perfect before we can do it, which you guessed it, it prevents us from doing it altogether. We often try to be at 100%, but there is benefit in being at 60% or 35% too. So start where you are, and give to yourself from where you are. Just get started. Have fun creating the morning ritual of your dreams.

PARENTS AND CAREGIVERS

People often ask me how to practice self-care with children. The question is interesting to me because of what it implies about parenting or caregiving. It implies that this role is something that never gives you space to do it. It also implies that taking care of yourself is something that you just do not do. It also implies this sort of constant struggle with energy. Now, I am not saying all those things aren't true to a certain extent, especially with very young children who require around the clock attention and care. But I think that we often put things on our children because they are a convenient excuse. Like who would argue that you are tired because of having children? When I was teaching, I went through something similar. If I said I was too tired to go out or do something, everyone was like, 'Well yes, she is a teacher...' It is as if it was justified.

I actually started my self-care journey after I had my first child. During the time after birth, I experienced postpartum depression and completely did not feel like myself. My daughter became the impetus for me to commit to my self-care, and to prioritize my wellbeing. Here's the thing though: Your children are not stopping you from doing self-care. We often confuse the responsibility of parenting with conscious choices that have nothing to do with parenting. It is why people without children also struggle with self -care and well-being. This is not just parents and caregivers who experience this, but I find that parents and caregivers constantly struggle with these things as they get on this self- care journey. If you are a parent or caregiver, consider this about your self- care practices:

1. They have a hard time asking for help. I know you have seen the scene where the woman is cleaning, and cooking, and taking care of the children. She is looking ragged while her husband is sitting on the couch. When he asks her what is wrong, she complains about all that she is doing. The husband says, 'All you had to do was ask,' while she fumes. This can feel infuriating, and I have found myself in this position before, but it is true. If you don't make the request, you can't expect someone to fill it, even if it is obvious. Also, I found that my husband didn't want to step in because whenever he tried, I would micro-manage and not trust him to do it. So he just waited until I asked him to do something. So much of self -care is finding the courage to deal with yourself differently so you can ask others to do the same. And without taking things off of your plate, making self- care a consistent practice can be difficult.

2. There is a struggle with saying no to their child or the person they are caregiving for. I know I definitely

struggle with this. Sometimes you have to say 'no', or 'not right now' to requests from your children. Clinical psychologist and parent expert, Dr. Becky has some great advice for this, and offers helpful perspective. It is okay not to play with your children all the time.[18] It actually models for them that it is okay to pass on wanting to do something. But we sometimes don't set up our family to support the self- care practices we so desperately need. It is important to get this to be all hands on deck.

3. Another struggle is having patience. If you have been burning out in your parenting and caregiver role, it is going to take some time to unbundle and understand how it happened, and to find strategies for not doing it that way again. So much of your aversion to self-care and wellbeing is rooted in old stories, triggers, and beliefs that we inherited earlier in our lives. This kind of patience is at tension with the constant train of responsibilities that call our name as parents and caregivers. And not giving ourselves that grace is detrimental to us as parents and caregivers.

Small steps.

Small steps have a great impact. I remember when I was not going outside, and I knew that being outside would help with my depression. I was staying at home with my daughter and

---

[18] Kennedy, Dr. Becky [@drbeckyatgoodinside]. *Instagram. https://www.instagram.com/drbeckyatgoodinside*

because of my husband's job, it could be several days straight without any break or reprieve. Instead of setting some unrealistic goal to go and walk for thirty minutes, I had a goal to go for a walk to get the mail. It gave me a goal to check the mail, and it got me walking for about five to seven minutes. I did this for quite some time, just going outside to check the mail. A few weeks later, I changed the mail route and walked around the apartment complex for an additional five minutes before making my way to the mailbox. After a few months, I would go for a walk and not even check the mail. This time was so restorative, but it took time to get into a routine. But those first small steps were what helped me finally get out of the rut.

When you are parenting or caregiving, doing things are on a minute by minute basis. Make it easier on yourself. Instead of feeling guilty that you can't do a self- care practice for a certain amount of time, start where you are. This is not about finding more time. It is about rearranging and using what you have. So often we start self- care in a deficit mode with our time. This is like a child coming to kindergarten, and a teacher yelling at them for not knowing how to read yet. So much of self- care practices is learning how to love the time we have as we make space for more time to become available to us.

One way to make more time is not to overschedule weekends. We can allow space for ourselves and our children to not be doing something at every moment. This practice of decluttering the calendar can be a great way to model self-care to our children. Designate certain Saturdays out of the month where you are staying in or relaxing without a plan. It does not need to be back to back things on the weekend. Of course, this goes back to setting boundaries that we talked about earlier and saying 'no.' But remember in doing this, you are showing and modeling for your children how to do the same thing when they get older and must make decisions about their own calendars. Managing energy means managing our calendars, and being realistic about what will happen if we expend our energy in this way without any time to recharge. This might totally shift how you think about your family's schedule and activities.

Self- care is a community effort. Taking care of yourself can have positive effects on your family. Taking care of yourself helps you to manage stress, and managing that stress inevitably makes you a happier, joyful parent and caregiver. We often think about the negative effects on our families if we say no or delegate, but we can relinquish control so we can find ourselves again

We have to start seeing ourselves as central to our family structure, rather than a machine. If we go down, it will affect all other parts of that structure. But we also need mechanisms in place so that our systems do not get overtaxed with trying to do too much. We need processes in places to distribute and manage how things flow and move around us.

I also want to name something super important: People will not do things exactly how you want, and that is okay. As you learn to let go of doing it all, you also have to let go of how it will get done. You have to give people the grace to help you and adjust. It is a learning process for everyone. I remember talking to my therapist about this. She reminded me that the fact was that I needed the help with things around the house. I was grappling with hiring someone to clean the house, and also in delegating more to my husband and parents. She asked, "Will the house cleaners clean the house exactly how you want?"

I quietly said, "No."

She then followed that up with another question. "And is that okay?"

I hesitantly said, "Yes."

But it was true that it may not be exactly how I might want it, but it will get done. Honestly, that was the biggest reason I was not letting things go; this need to try to control everything. If my husband makes dinner, he might dirty more dishes than I would, but for thirty minutes I get to breathe or play with my children without feeling overwhelmed with trying to do it all. But it is okay not to have things done exactly how I want; this is how we break cycles. We constantly keep asking, 'Is this working?' And if the answer is no, then we can work through things differently. It is learning to reorient the balance to floating instead of splashing around all the time and expending too much energy. Focus. We have to learn to focus on the most important things, and that in and of itself is the most important form of taking care of our wellbeing on a consistent basis.

On legacy

Developing your self- care practices can be a lesson in helping your children, and other family members, to develop their own rituals. When I have quiet time in the morning, I also encourage my daughter to do the same thing. I am teaching her that I have boundaries that are beautiful, and I am also teaching her to make time for self- care. A legacy of self- care keeps me anchored when life feels like a whirlwind. Taking care of yourself is a powerful testament to your values and beliefs, which can have a profound effect on your family in so many ways.

CONCLUSION

We are at the end of the book, and I am grateful that you took this time to put yourself first.

I hope that this book has given you something more than just practical self- care tips. I hope that it has given you a new or refreshed perspective about your value, and the necessity for you to nurture yourself in ways that matter. As you continue your self- care journey, keep these three things in mind:

1. Be generous with yourself. Give yourself the time, effort, resources, and tenderness that you give so gracefully to others. Make plans to do things that you enjoy, and luxuriate in the time that you spend on restoring and reclaiming your self- care practices.

Here are few ideas that you might do immediately:

- When you receive a gift card, spend it on something frivolous. Don't overthink what you should buy, and get what you really desire.
- Use gifts you receive. You do not need to wait until it is a good time to indulge in a product, or to wear an outfit. Now is always a good time.

- When you run errands, take five minutes to breathe or meditate before you go into the store.
- When you can't do something, simply say 'no' and don't apologize. Being busy does not need an apology.
- Put your phone on 'do not disturb' before you go to bed.
- What is an item you need? Make plans to get it for yourself in the next 30-60 days.
- Get an accountability buddy who will check in on you about being generous to yourself.

Generosity to yourself is a practice. The more you practice it, the easier it becomes to do. Every single day ask yourself: 'How can I be generous to myself? How can I remember that I am worth the effort? How can I remind myself that I am allowed to put me first?'

2. Have fun. This life is meant for more than working hard. You have a life of joy that is waiting if you to notice it. When self- care starts to feel boring, add more play to your practices. Joy is a powerful tool. Notice what makes you feel fantastic and do more of it.

3. Embrace curiosity. We talked a lot about curiosity in this book, and I want to reiterate it here. Curiosity over judgement is how you will learn to embrace all of you. Allow curiosity to take you down a path that honors your creativity and light. Continue to unearth parts of yourself, and unfold the beauty that is you and your life.

I hope you find exactly what you need as you deepen into your self- care journey. I hope that feelings of guilt are replaced with feelings of goodness. I hope that you create a master-piece of a life that centers your care. May your being well be the catalyst for increased abundance and love in your life.

Keep showing up. Keep being curious. Keep giving yourself grace.

Keep practicing self- care all the time.

RESOURCES

This is a list of resources that guide how I approach self-care. This list is not exhaustive, rather a sample of resources that have been impactful on my own self-care journey.

Cameron, Julia. *The Artist's Way: A Spiritual Path to Higher Creativity.* New York: J.P. Tarcher/Putnam, 2002.

May, Katherine. *Wintering: The Power of Rest and Retreat in Difficult Times.* Cengage Gale, 2021. Print.

Walker, Alice. *In Search of Our Mothers' Gardens.* Mariner Books, 2003. Print.

Hershey, Tricia. *The Nap Ministry*, 25 Mar. 2021, https://thenapministry.wordpress.com/.

Lewis, Shantrelle P., *In Our Mothers' Gardens.* House of the Seven Sisters, 2020, Netflix, www.netflix.com/title/81354661.

CPSIA information can be obtained
at www.ICGtesting.com
Printed in the USA
LVHW022007261221
707061LV00003B/135

9 781951 943790